#staymarried
A Couple's Devotional

#staymarried

A Couple's Devotional

30-Minute Weekly Devotions to Grow in Faith and Joy from I Do to Ever After

MICHELLE PETERSON

ALTHEA
PRESS

This book is dedicated to the greatest man I've ever known, my husband, Tony. Thank you for continuing to choose me.

This book is also for my daughters: Claire Elaine, Nora Kate, and Alice Jane. Someday the world will try to convince you that you are incomplete outside of marriage. That's ridiculous. Someday someone will try to convince you that they love you, but they won't treat you as well as your father treats me. Don't fall for it. You are incredible young women, strong and brave, made to love and be loved extravagantly. Your father and I are eternally proud of you.

Contents

He loved her, of course,
but better than that,
he chose her, day after day.
Choice: that was the thing.

—*Sherman Alexie,* The Toughest Indian in the World

Introduction

My fifth year of marriage to my husband, Tony, was a turning point for me. After living in the Midwest for three years, we'd returned to our home in the Pacific Northwest, eager to be near family and reconnect with old friends. Before we moved away, we'd been a part of a vibrant and growing church community, one filled with authentic, messy people who were full of love for each other and love for us. These people taught us what it was to have a true partner in life, nurtured us through the beginning of our relationship, blessed us on our wedding day, and encouraged us as newlyweds. That's what we thought we would return to, like a warm and loving childhood home. Instead, we came home to splintered relationships, infidelity, and divorce.

Couples who had been married for decades were now living in separate homes. Newlyweds whose gifts I hadn't gotten around to shipping were already broken up. I could no longer keep track of the number of phone calls, text messages, and e-mails I'd received from friends telling me that their husband or wife was leaving them. That they'd been cheated on or been unfaithful. I'd been told, as we all have, that the divorce rate in the United States hovers around 50 percent, but now that number had real people attached to them—people besides my own parents.

My mother and father separated when I was just three years old. Their divorce was final by the time I was five, and then I didn't lay eyes on my father again until I was an adult. My younger sister and I were raised by our incredibly determined and independent single mother. I spent my childhood as her confidant, wiping her tears when her boyfriends broke off their relationships, or when she found out they were married, or when the wife she knew about found out about her. Once in a while, a boyfriend would stick around long enough to move in and pretend to be my dad. Then it would end. It always ended. We'd move back in with my grandparents until my mom became too determined and independent to accept their help, and then we'd move out and start the cycle all over again.

I share this background to tell you that the odds that I would stay married were not in my favor. Children of divorce are more likely to get divorced as adults than those who don't come from a divorced home. Research also indicates that people are at greater risk for divorce if they experience depression, as well as if they were sexually abused as children, both of which are true of me.

My husband, my rock, comes into our marriage with none of these challenges. His parents are still married, and he has no history of depression or abuse of any kind. I, on the other hand, carry these black marks in my heart, marks I didn't ask for or bring upon myself. I know that a lot of you carry them as well.

So in our fifth year of marriage, as I consoled so many friends about their breakups, I became more and more restless. Their devastating stories were reminders that the stats were stacked against me, against all of us. The reality of how fragile marriage really is kept me awake at night. I'd roll over on my tear-soaked pillow searching for my husband's face in the dark, pleading with him for reassurance. He did his best to remind me of his love, his commitment, but it didn't feel like enough. I had become keenly aware that I was not immune to the possibility of divorce.

The hashtag #staymarried was born out of my hopeful questions. Will Tony and I stay married? What does it take to stay married? I wasn't satisfied with clichéd answers such as "A great marriage puts God first." I knew too many couples, including many who put their trust in God, who'd watched their marriages crumble underneath their feet. I needed to know more. I needed to know the science and psychology as well as the spiritual reality of the forces that can either pull us together or drive us apart.

As I began to research for myself and share the findings with others, I began to sleep better. I started to understand ways to defy the odds, and I wanted everyone to be equipped with the same marriage-boosting knowledge, especially newlyweds. "Stay married" is not a command or a stance against divorce. I don't believe it's healthy to stay married to an abuser, an addict, or a narcissist. I recognize that, as painful as it may be, divorce is sometimes the best possible decision. Still, I see now that it doesn't have to be inevitable for any of us.

This book is my invitation to you, an invitation to discovery and to faithfulness. With each reading, I hope you discover more about yourself and more about your partner. By committing to weekly reading and discussion, I hope you build a habit of faithfulness. Faithfulness, after all, can only be measured over the course of time. It can't be rushed. If we want to have marriages that are strong enough to weather whatever life throws at us, we can't take any shortcuts.

These devotions are our stories, our attempts to use the data that's out there and love each other in a way that brings hope and light and a chance for all of us to push against the stats that hover over us. I'm not a therapist, or a scientist, or a social worker. The only qualification I have is hope. My hope is that you'll find encouragement in these pages and that you'll use this book to build a foundation for your own efforts to #staymarried.

How to Use This Book

This book is made up of 52 weekly devotions. The best way to use it is to start with your calendar. Schedule 30 to 60 minutes each week to read and discuss it with your partner, and don't let anything or anyone else take that time away from you. Prioritize connecting with your partner via the Scripture, reading, and discussion questions.

Keep a Bible and a journal close by. Some weeks will include instructions for additional Bible reading, and journaling your answers to the questions, whether separately or together, can help you reflect on your thoughts each week and serve as a record of your takeaways at the end of the year.

Slower Is Better

These 52 devotions are meant to be read together with your spouse over the course of one year. You could binge read this book. Go ahead; devour it. If I were you, that's exactly what I would do—but that's because I'm impatient. One of the gifts I hope you'll receive in this devotional is the gift of pace. A marriage is more like a marathon than a sprint, and if we're going to make it to the finish line, we need to learn to pace ourselves.

So when you and your spouse use the book together, try to talk about only one devotion per week. In order to really grow, we need to give ourselves time to reflect and put into practice what we've learned. As James 1:22 says, "Put the word into action. If you think hearing is what matters most, you are going to find you have been deceived." If you and your spouse devour this book without giving yourself time to let the words sink in—both the words I've written for you and your words to each other—you'll walk away without really letting the ideas penetrate your consciousness. These devotions are meant to be relatively quick reads. The discussion questions and the natural flow of conversation and discovery that happen *after* the reading are what's meant to draw you closer together. If it takes more than the 30 to 60 minutes you've allowed yourself, keep going. Work through any tough discussions together as best you can and continue to keep communication open all week.

Grow in Faithfulness

Along with pace, I hope this book will help you receive the gift of developing a faithful habit. Faithfulness is only discovered over time. Anyone can do one nice thing or even a few nice things in a row, but a faithful person is one who consistently does the right thing, no matter the circumstances, over and over and over again. Since faithfulness is the cornerstone of a long-lasting marriage, I hope you'll practice being faithful to this work week after week. Make your marriage a priority now so that you can reap the rewards of building a marriage you love for years to come.

Reading Alone

Ideally, this book would bring you and your partner closer together. But I know what it's like to be in a season where only one of you wants to grow in your relationship. If that's you, I invite you to read this book and journal your thoughts on your own. As you develop a deeper sense of love and perhaps some new perspectives, your partner may become interested in joining you. But even if they don't, you'll still benefit from doing the work on your own.

Reading with a Group

Being a part of a community of people who are all heading in the same direction is great for your marriage. If you're reading this book with a group, or leading such a group, make sure you look ahead and choose the weeks that best fit your group dynamic. If you're longtime friends, you may be able to have discussions on intimacy and baggage without any trouble. But if the group members are fairly new to each other, you may want to choose weeks that are less emotionally draining while still being points of growth. Feel free to skip around and use the subjects that work best for you.

Pray for Each Other

Beginning and ending each week in prayer is a wonderful way to slow yourself down and prepare your heart to receive something new. Whether you hold hands and pray aloud, meditate silently, or use any other variation of prayer, don't neglect this essential unifying practice. I am praying for you.

Planning a Beautiful Marriage

Like most girls, her imagination carried her
just as far as the altar and no further.
—Margaret Mitchell, Gone with the Wind

May He grant the dreams of your heart and
see your plans through to the end.
—Psalm 20:4

I love weddings—the gown, the music, the venue, the cake. Planning a wedding is dreamy. I get excited for my newly engaged friends, but I worry for them, too. I wonder if, among all the details of planning their wedding, they've made room for planning their marriage.

Many couples spend months, sometimes years, planning for their special day without much thought about the day after. And I'm certain that when two people stand in front of each other wearing the nicest clothes they've ever worn, being stared at by everyone they know, they do not imagine ever getting a divorce. According to a 2012 Clark University poll, 86 percent of people ages 18–29 who get married imagine they will be together for the rest of their lives. Statistics also tell us that only half of them will be.

The truth is that it's not enough to merely want to be together forever. Forever, it turns out, is a really long time. During forever, we might lose jobs, have babies, lose babies, buy a home, get foreclosed on, get in car accidents, age, become less attractive, cut carbs, binge on alcohol, burn dinner, and yell at each other. As overwhelming as wedding planning can be, getting married is not nearly as difficult as staying married. (And, as I've witnessed time and time again, divorce is even harder.) We live in a society determined to sell us on every single detail of the wedding, from the color of the bridesmaid dresses to the flavor of the icing on the cake. Unfortunately, not nearly as much emphasis is placed on helping us develop the skills and characteristics necessary to build a marriage that will last.

If I could give all engaged couples a marriage planning checklist, it would be the 10 suggestions given next. And even if you're reading this after you've said your "I dos," go through this list and think about each item. Because after your one-time big event, there is a lifelong relationship that will need constant attention, and what matters in the end is the way you and your spouse handle that relationship.

1 **Spend time with each other's families.** Eat meals together, watch movies, play games. Your partner's family is about to be your family. For better or worse, it's a package deal,

so it's worth your time to learn their unique family culture as much as possible before they become your in-laws.

2   **Read a book about marriage together.** There are tons of great resources to choose from, but the point of reading a book about marriage together is to talk through your own thoughts on the content—two people can read the exact same text and come away with completely different ideas. Focusing on a book can help you dig a little deeper into the ideas you might not think to share in your everyday lives.

3   **Spend time with your friends.** When you're crazy in love, it's easy to forget that anyone in the world exists except your incredible and unique partner. But before this big love happened, you had friends. Don't forget about them! Make every effort to spend time with them, with or without your partner. Marriages succeed in community and fail in isolation. Maintaining a close community of people is one of the best things you can do to ensure your marriage lasts beyond the honeymoon phase.

4   **Talk about money.** Money is one of the top five issues couples fight about most. Though it may make for awkward conversation, take the opportunity *before* you're married to share the details of your finances, money habits, hopes, and goals. Try your best to suspend judgment; this is a fantastic opportunity to grow together.

5   **Talk about your views on divorce.** Do either of you believe there are reasons to get divorced? What would cause you to throw in the towel? Did you experience the divorce of your own parents (or other family members) growing up? What was that like for you?

6   **Get in some fights.** Really. Make sure you've had a hand-
    ful of fights, and then talk about the way you fight. Much
    of marriage is navigating conflict and stresses, and some
    conflict is a natural part of any close relationship. It's
    important to learn how to handle it without avoiding it.

7   **Talk about intimacy issues.** Talk about any past partners.
    Has either of you experienced any abuse? Do you watch
    pornography? Do you have any fears about intimacy?
    Any hopes?

8   **Talk about church and your spiritual beliefs.** What is
    important to you about your faith and your lifestyle? Are
    you keeping the traditions you were raised with, or will you
    forge new ones? If your beliefs differ drastically, can you
    still respect one another and remain open to the other's
    perspective? Or are you each hoping the other will change?
    Be honest about how you feel and what you really want.

9   **Discuss politics.** In polite society, it might be best to avoid
    these topics, but it's crucial to talk about them with your
    spouse. Your marriage should be a safe place where you
    can say what you really think and process how you feel
    about what's going on in the world. You should be able to
    bring up questions and concerns about politics with your
    partner without fear of getting in a fight. As when discuss-
    ing religion, can you respect one another and remain open
    to the other's perspective?

10 **Don't go into debt for your wedding.** You'll avoid a lot
    of post-wedding arguments and stress by not going into
    debt for the wedding. Your guests probably won't even
    notice the thread count of the napkins or the vintage of the

champagne. Don't spend all your time and money on things that won't make an impact on your marriage.

Whether your wedding's a backyard potluck or a grand ballroom soirée, the shortsightedness of wedding planning doesn't do much to equip you for the road ahead. Your views on some things will probably change over time and with experience, but your ability to verbally work through your thoughts with one another will give you a solid foundation for a lifetime of celebrating long after your big party.

For Discussion:

1   Look through the preceding list. Which of the items have you already worked through?
2   Are there items on this list you haven't talked about yet? Talk through some of these items now, and make plans to work through the rest.
3   If you've already had your wedding, what were your favorite moments of that day? Share with one another.
4   If you're still looking forward to your wedding, what do you imagine will be most important to you? Why?

Week 2

For Better or Worse

> *God is not a man—He doesn't lie.*
> *God isn't the son of a man to want to take*
> *back what He's said, Or say something and not*
> *follow through, or speak and not act on it.*
> *—Numbers 23:19*

I love weddings. Have I mentioned that yet? Not to play favorites, but the best wedding I've ever attended was the one my own husband, Tony, officiated for our friends George and Erika.

Tony normally has no fear of speaking in front of a crowd, but performing a wedding was a little intimidating. He was particularly worried about the vows. You see, George and Erika are not exactly traditional. I don't know any other couple whose engagement photos featured the groom holding a live chicken while the bride stood beside him holding an ax. Tony wanted them to have vows as unique and quirky as they were.

In lieu of a big rehearsal, Tony presented George and Erika with traditional vows over dinner in our home. He led them through the practice round while they held hands, gazed at each other, and repeated Tony's words. They beamed with love and admiration for each other. When they finished, Tony handed them each a pen. "Change whatever you want," he said. "This is your wedding, and we want these vows to be yours."

George and Erika looked at each other and shrugged. "I don't have anything," Erika said.

"Neither do I," George said. "I think they're perfect."

They beamed some more, and I don't think either of them caught the surprised looks on our faces. It turns out vows don't need to be unique—they just need to be honest.

A few days later, George and Erika exchanged those vows, words that have been recited between husbands and wives over many generations. *I take you, my beloved, to have and to hold from this day forward, for better or for worse, in sickness and in health, to love and to cherish, all the days of my life.* This, or some version of it, is the promise we all make when we marry. To take the whole person, not just the parts we like. To love them on their hardest days, not just their happiest. To believe in them when they don't believe in themselves. To honor them even when they act dishonorably. As I take another look at these words, I notice nothing in the language that says "unless." There is no caveat for our day-to-day emotions. There is no exit route in case either spouse loses their job, their motivation, or their health.

Watching my husband lead George and Erika through the ceremony opened my eyes to something more. It hit me that by making this promise to each other, they were touching on something holy. Throughout Scripture, when God speaks, his words are a promise, a vow, and a covenant between himself and his people. His words are to be taken as utter truth, unbound by time, and as unbreakable commitments.

He promised Noah he would never again destroy the earth with a flood. He promised Abraham, who was almost a hundred years old and still didn't have a child of his own, that his descendants would outnumber the stars. God's nature is to keep his word, and in exchanging vows—in making promises right at the beginning of this long journey of marriage—we touch on this holy characteristic. A promise kept is the very essence of commitment; it is a seed sprouting and cultivating trust, the evidence of love as a verb and not a noun. "For better or worse," we say.

For better. That means when Erika is in a good mood. When she shines radiantly with love for George. When she is kind and funny, just the way he likes her. When George is thoughtful and responsible. When he is simultaneously affectionate and sarcastic, just the way she likes him.

For worse. That means when Erika is disrespectful and selfish. When she is tired and irritable. When she feels insecure and acts jealously. When George is thoughtless and rude. When he betrays her and disregards her feelings. When he is arrogant and prideful.

For better or worse. We're committing to take each other not only as we stand on our wedding day, but through all of the changes that we will inevitably go through. We discover that the promise we made on that magical day is not as easy to keep as it was to say. It is in the gap between making the promise and keeping it that we find this holy process, the refining work of asking ourselves, "Did we really mean it?" The daily work of keeping that promise helps us understand a bit more about the nature of God, who is gracious, forgiving, and patient. In our humanity, we hope for *better*. But it is through *worse* that we discover our true capacity to love.

For Discussion:

1 Take another look at your wedding vows. Did you go for something traditional, write your own, or a mixture of the two? What influenced how you handled your wedding vows?

2 With your vows in hand, take a few moments to reread and renew your vows to one another. Meditate on the meaning of these words and how the meaning may have changed for you since you first said these words to one another.

3 If you're not yet married, how do you imagine you'll handle your own wedding vows? Talk through what's most important to you.

Confession

> *So own up to your sins to one another and pray*
> *for one another. In the end, you may be healed.*
> *Your prayers are powerful when they are rooted*
> *in a righteous life.*
> *—James 5:16*

Once, when I was six, my younger sister and I were playing the game all children know without being taught: the lava game. We jumped and chased each other, trying not to touch the imaginary lava on the floor . . . until I slipped and cracked the coffee table in half. I scrambled to reassemble it, digging an empty box of Frosted Flakes out of the garbage and propping it up so that it held the two halves of the table together. Then I covered the massive crack with strategically placed magazines and hoped my mom would never find out.

But a little while later, my mom instructed me to "get that box out from under the coffee table." She watched me reach for the box, then gasped when the table fell and magazines scattered everywhere. I tried to look surprised, but I'll bet I just looked guilty. I don't exactly remember what happened next, but I'm sure it wasn't pleasant.

When you're not six years old anymore, it's easy to see how ridiculous that plan was. Did I think I could keep that cereal box under the table forever? I knew I'd be in trouble, but all I could do was avoid the consequences for a couple of hours.

As adults, we can sometimes manage to avoid consequences for a little longer than that. We might be able to keep a secret and move on with life. However, what we cannot hide from is our God-given conscience. The weight of guilt, the cover-up, and the little white lies can be exhausting. And in the case of our marriages, though we may think we're hurting only ourselves, secrets have other consequences.

Secrets and Consequences

Have you ever kept a secret from your spouse? Did you muster up the courage to confess? Often, when someone says they have a confession to make, the next thing they say can be hard to hear. My friend Holly told me once that she'd been on the receiving end of a confession from her husband. She could tell he'd had something on his mind all day, and as they got ready for bed that night, he said the fateful words: "Holly, I have a confession." Ready for the worst, she braced herself. "I bought steaks out of a guy's trunk today," he admitted.

"The guy who was outside our house last week trying to sell you steaks? The guy we said no to?"

"Yeah," her husband said. "I saw him again, and this time I caved and bought them."

Relieved and thankful, Holly laughed. "No big deal," she said. "It was just 30 dollars' worth of meat."

Regular confession is necessary because we make mistakes regularly. Regardless of how insignificant Holly's husband's secret was, he was already dealing with the guilt of keeping something from his wife. He could have gotten away with this one, but I love that he confessed! I love that he didn't hold on to it, convincing himself it was none of her business. I love that she laughed. I love that, as they make confession a common practice, they will continue to develop trust and intimacy. When we try to hide our mistakes from our spouses, we diminish the possibilities for intimacy. We can never truly experience the blessing of knowing and being known when we keep parts of ourselves covered up.

Of course, there will be times when a confession won't be so easy. If you're keeping a secret you know you should confess, here are a few things that might help.

Making the Best of Your Confession

1 **Good timing.** A drive-by confession—one made as your husband is heading out the door for work or as your wife is in the middle of a big project—is selfish. Make sure you have time to talk, time for your spouse to absorb, and time to ask and answer any questions.

2 **Full disclosure.** Avoid confessing only the things you might get caught for and leaving out the details your spouse is not likely to find out. Trust comes from honesty, and deciding your spouse doesn't deserve the whole truth is just as dishonest as the secret you're keeping in the first place.

3 **Ask for forgiveness.** Ask for forgiveness humbly, not only for whatever you confess but also for keeping secrets at all. Know that as you ask for forgiveness, you hold your spouse under no obligation to extend mercy.

4 **No excuses.** Don't thwart your own confession by making excuses for your actions. The worst thing you can say is, "I'm sorry, *but . . . .*" Instead, just say, "I'm sorry for what I did. Will you forgive me?" If your spouse has questions, offer an explanation, but make sure your explanation isn't also an attempt to be let off the hook. In order for trust to grow, you need to own your mistakes and not lay blame on your spouse to make yourself feel better.

While confessing to one another can be a painful process, it will result in higher levels of trust for both of you. It's my hope that you're reading this book because you want to stay married, and it's tough to stay married when you're keeping secrets from each other.

For Discussion:

1 Have you ever had the "Here are all my past secrets" conversation with your spouse? If you have and there's anything you held back, this is a good time to confess.

2 If you've shared all the big stuff, are there little things you've withheld from each other? Try this with your partner today: "Honey, I don't want to have secrets between us. I feel like I should tell you _____."

3   The Bible tells us we should make confession a "common
     practice" and that we will receive healing from confessing
     often. Discuss what this means to each of you.

4   We'll talk about this next week, but in the meantime, how
     do you think you can create a safe environment in your
     marriage for confession to be a common practice?

Week 4

Safety Net

> **Peter:** *"Lord, when someone has sinned against me, how many times ought I forgive him? Once? Twice? As many as seven times?"*
> **Jesus:** *"You must forgive not seven times, but seventy times seven."*
> —Matthew 18:21–22

If communication is key to a healthy marriage, then keeping secrets is key to destroying one. Last week, I shared about the dangers of keeping secrets and the power of regular confession with your spouse. Now I'd like to touch on the other side of the issue: receiving a confession.

When your spouse makes a mistake or offends you, you have the opportunity either to act self-righteous or to make your marriage a safety net. When you're on the receiving end of your spouse's blunder, it's natural to become indignant: "I'm right. You're wrong. You owe me." But that stance, however natural, puts you at odds with your spouse instead of pursuing unity. So what can you do instead?

First of all, if your spouse is willing to confess their error to you, it signifies their desire to be closer, to own up to their mistakes, and to repair what is broken. As hard as it might be to listen to a confession, it's much more divisive to have secrets between the two of you. If your spouse starts a conversation with "Honey, I have a confession to make," let your first reaction be to take a deep breath. Remember that a confession is a good thing.

Then, listen. Think about what your loved one is saying. Try not to jump to conclusions or add words to their confession. Take another deep breath. Receiving a confession can be painful, so don't discount that. But ask yourself, "Do I want our marriage to be a safety net?" I hope you do.

When your marriage is a safety net, you can fall into it with peace and security. But your marriage is not a safe place when it's full of grudges and lists of past mistakes that are picked up again whenever a new mistake is made. We have to be conscious of what we're doing to either foster a sense of safety or diminish it. If we want our marriages to be safety nets, we need to quickly and completely forgive the little things that come up.

For example, say my husband forgets to grab some milk on his way home from work, and I respond by saying, "Of course you forgot the milk. You forgot our anniversary last year, so why would I think you could remember milk?" That response should make you cringe! Not only was I snarky, I used his small mistake to bring up other mistakes that have nothing to do with the milk but that I've clearly not forgiven. Do you think he'd feel safe around me after that? Do you think he'd feel loved? Not likely. If we want to create safety nets for our spouses, we must extend grace.

In your marriage, how often do you recall past grievances in a new argument? How likely are you to use phrases like "I knew you'd do that!" or "You always . . ." or "You never . . ."? If we give our partners a hard time over every little thing, we create expectations of perfection that no one can live up to. This makes it difficult for our spouses to do something that is already difficult: confess. We have to love our spouses before, during, and especially after the little confessions, so that when the big confessions come, we're in a better place to receive them.

The Safety-Net Way of Receiving a Confession:

1. **Listen with love.** When my husband confesses to me, I try to put myself in the position of his protector and guardian before I allow myself to take his offense personally. When I decide I have the opportunity to show him love, especially when he's embarrassed or ashamed, it opens the door for more communication instead of less.

2. **Give the benefit of the doubt.** As you listen, think about whether or not your spouse intended to hurt you. Most of the time, you can give them the benefit of the doubt and believe the best about them.

3. **Get clarity.** This one can be hard to do, so give yourself some time. If you need space away from your spouse after hearing their confession, ask for it. If you have a lot

of questions, ask them. Get clarity on whatever is going through your mind. The stories we make up on our own can often be much worse than the reality of what happened.

4 **Get healing.** If you're Holly from last week's example, and your husband confessed to purchasing steaks, you likely stopped at step two and moved on. However, if your spouse confesses to a bigger betrayal, you may have more work to do. Consider counseling if that's appropriate for you. A good counselor can help you see each other from a third perspective and offer practical steps toward healing after a betrayal.

Marriage is not for the faint of heart. My hope and prayer for you is that you never have something severe to confess and that you never have to be on the receiving end of a hurtful secret. However, the reality is that it's much more important for us to figure out how to navigate secrets and confessions than to spend our energy avoiding them altogether.

For Discussion:

1 Have you ever been forgiven for something you'd done wrong? How did that feel?

2 Have you ever had the opportunity to forgive some-one? Did your forgiveness make a difference in that relationship?

3   Are you holding onto little grudges in your marriage now? Confess them to each other and make the choice to release them.

4   Read Matthew 18:21–35. Talk together about what you think it means. What is Jesus asking us to do? Why do you think it matters?

5   Pray. Thank God for his great forgiveness found in the life, death, and resurrection of Jesus Christ. Ask for his protection over your marriage and his healing work in your hearts as you work to create a safety-net atmosphere in your marriage.

Battle Buddies

> *It is not good for the man to be alone, so I will create*
> *a companion for him, a perfectly suited partner.*
> —*Genesis 2:18*

I was raised to believe that, as a woman, I could accomplish anything. My mother modeled this belief with her own life. As a divorcée from the time I was three, she managed to earn three master's degrees and had a long career as an immigration inspector, one of the few females in a male-dominated field. My mother was strong and smart and wouldn't be pushed around.

When I became a Christian at 22, I found myself surrounded by a bunch of wedding-crazed young women I didn't understand. Getting married wasn't even on my radar, but in my church, they were still teaching that it was the greatest aspiration a woman could have. I was supposed to believe I was created by God and that his big plan for my life was that I would be somebody else's "helpmeet"? Something seemed off.

Have you heard the term "helpmeet" before? It comes from the King James Version of the Bible's rendering of Genesis 2:18: "And the Lord God said, It is not good that the man should be alone; I will make him a help meet for him." As I learned from John and Stasi Eldredge's book *Captivating*, the original Hebrew phrase—translated variously as "helpmeet," "companion," and "helper"—is *ezer kenegdo*, a term Hebrew scholar Robert Alter calls "notoriously difficult to translate." (He himself has settled on "sustainer beside him.")

That first word, *ezer*, is used about 20 other times in the Old Testament, and in every other instance, the person being described as a "helper" is God himself. It's translated as "protects" in Deuteronomy 33:29, which says God is "the shield that protects" Israel, and as "help" in Psalm 121:1–2, which says, "I look up at the vast size of the mountains—from where will my help come in times of trouble? The Eternal Creator of heaven and earth and these mountains will send the help I need." These verses describe life-and-death situations in which God is our only hope. Maybe a better translation of *ezer* would be "lifesaver."

Kenegdo means "alongside," "opposite to," or "counterpart." These alternate translations for the same Hebrew words build a fuller picture of God's original design.

EZER	KENEGDO
lifesaver	alongside
sustainer	counterpart
rescuer	facing

So despite what I was learning from my friends at age 22 about the idea of the helpmeet as a meek sidekick picking up socks and making sandwiches, what I've come to understand about the phrase *ezer kenegdo* is that it looks much more like a partner, a co-warrior, or a battle buddy.

Battle Buddies

My friend Zech (pronounced "Zak") used to be an airborne medic in the Army, and he has plenty of crazy stories about that time, with a lot of devastation and heartache, but also brotherhood and camaraderie. He shared with me that the core of his Army training was trust and teamwork. Before they could ever go into battle together, it was essential that each guy knew he could fully rely on the soldier next to him.

Zech's first experience with this concept was getting off the bus with 30 other recruits and being told to stand in a line together, side by side, about an arm's length apart. A rucksack with a bunch of equipment was tossed in front of each of them, and they were told to pack everything into their sacks quickly and efficiently. At the signal, the soldiers fell to the ground and got to work. One by one, each soldier stood up when his pack was full and zipped. The drill sergeant would then walk over to a standing soldier, unzip his pack, toss all the contents at his feet, and shout, "Do it again!"

This happened repeatedly, and, understandably, the soldiers got frustrated. What were they missing? How could they get this right? After several packs had been emptied and each soldier had been barked at repeatedly to start over, Zech figured it out. He finished his pack and, before standing up, started helping the guy on his left finish his pack, too. Other soldiers took note and did the same thing, and when all the packs were finished, all of the soldiers stood up at the same time. Only then, when they finished together, had they successfully completed their task.

Zech says this kind of thing happened all the time during training. Over and over, they were taught that they did not work alone, that they needed each other to complete everything from waxing floors to running miles. By the time these soldiers were on a mission in hostile territory, they were ready to fight with and for each other. They'd built trust by working side by side.

This is the way we need to think of our spouses. We build trust by working together. We are co-warriors, battle buddies, and eye-to-eye partners. We need to be able to work together in the mundane chores and activities of life to build that sense of trust and teamwork that will help us fight whatever greater battles we may face together.

For Discussion:

1   Was your parents' marriage one that demonstrated teamwork in all aspects, or one where each person had specific roles and responsibilities that they accomplished on their own? What did their marriage teach you about teamwork?

2   Have any of your spouse's qualities or characteristics blessed you in an essential way? When have you experienced them as a lifesaver, sustainer, or rescuer?

3   Ask your partner what they could use your help with this coming week.

4   Pray. Thank God for the gifts he has given you in your partner. Ask him to reveal to you how you can serve one another in greater ways.

To Nag and to Scold

It is better to dwell outside on the corner of your roof
than to live inside your house with a badgering wife.
—*Proverbs 25:24*

I have trouble asking for help. As an independent woman raised by an equally independent woman, I was very accustomed to doing things on my own before I got married. I was convinced that asking a man for help would necessarily involve begging or nagging, and I firmly believed that other people should be just as self-sufficient as I was—I wasn't going to put up with laziness in any relationship I was in! I had trouble imagining a partner who could freely ask for or offer help.

Early in our dating relationship, Tony was laid off from a job he'd had for six years. He was looking for work for the first time in a long time, and truthfully, he wasn't quite sure the best way to go about it. I, on the other hand, was a pro at finding work. I loved updating my résumé and applying for new jobs even when I was happy with my current employment. It frustrated me to see him stalled at the starting line, but I didn't want to nag him about it.

Then a light went on. I realized I'd never offered to help. Here I was, gainfully employed, watching silently as the man I loved floundered through his first real experience with unemployment. What if, instead of nagging him about getting a job, I could offer support?

With this new attitude, I simply told him, "I know you've been on these interviews with no luck. I love working on résumés and interview skills, and I would love to help you with yours if you're open to it."

As soon as the words came out of my mouth, I realized how silly it was that I'd spent all this time silently frustrated. He did want my help and truly welcomed my input. He didn't consider me a nag, but he also didn't want to burden me with his stress. Our relationship was still so new that we hadn't quite figured out how to help each other, or that helping each other is one of the great benefits of being in a relationship in the first place. It's easy to forget that God has created us to need each other and to rely on each other when we live in a culture that values independence and self-sufficiency above all else. I was learning to be his helper, his *ezer kenegdo*. In this case, I was pretty good at job searching, and Tony could benefit from my experience. Rather than nagging him about getting it done, I could offer my help and be a part of him soaring forward in his career.

Fast forward 10 years, and I still have an independent streak, which doesn't always work so well when you're married and part of a team. Sometimes I have to remind myself I need his help as much as he needs mine. I need to ask. I need to be patient.

Most wives would rather fulfill the role of "sustainer beside him" than "nag behind him." Here are five ways to make sure you're helping instead of nagging when something needs to get done.

1 **Ask kindly.** Try "Honey, would you mind taking out the trash?" instead of "The trash needs to go out, and it's your job to do it." Stop for a moment and consider: *Which would I respond better to, a command or a kind request?*

2 **Ask ahead of time.** "Babe, it doesn't need to happen right now, but can you make sure the trash gets taken to the curb before the garbage trucks come on Tuesday morning?" A little heads-up goes a long way.

3 **Ask how you can help.** "My love, it seems like we haven't gotten the trash out in time the last couple of weeks. Would you like me to take it out and you take over a different chore? Or is there a way I can remind you without feeling like a nag? Maybe we can put a reminder in your phone?" You're still being kind, you're still asking ahead of time, and now you're offering to be a part of the solution.

4 **Be grateful and appreciative.** "Tony, I appreciate how hard you work. I'm really proud of all that you've accomplished." This has nothing to do with the trash, but we need to show appreciation not just for the things on our task lists, but for who we are to each other. Most of us are inclined to do more than is asked of us when we know we are appreciated.

5 **Let it go.** I use "taking out the trash" as an example because in most households, it needs to get done. Friends, if you're waiting around for your partner to take out the trash, and you really don't want a stinky kitchen, roll up your sleeves

and take it out yourself. Marriage is teamwork, and this is one of the many times you will take on a task you might not like. Don't make your partner feel badly about it. Just take care of it. It's not worth it to speak condescendingly to your spouse over a small errand, chore, or favor.

The goal here is to be partners together, not to be the boss or make your beloved wish he lived on the corner of his roof far away from you. Think about not only the words you use but also how you feel when you approach each other. Think about the ways you can partner together to make both your lives better instead of treating each other as taskmasters and task performers. No task is more important than your connection with each other.

For Discussion:

1   How has being married changed your views on dependence versus independence?
2   In what ways do you look to each other for help?
3   Besides chores and daily tasks, what do you appreciate about each other? Be specific.
4   Pray. Ask for guidance so that the little tasks within your marriage don't distract you from God's greater purpose in your life together. Pray that he would cover you with a spirit of gentleness and of respect for each other.

Don't Fight over the Butter

*So I don't run aimlessly. I don't let my eyes
drift off the finish line. When I box, I don't
throw punches in the air.*
—*1 Corinthians 9:26*

At our wedding, Tony and I set out a small cigar box and little blank cards and asked our guests to share some advice for our marriage. Sometime after our honeymoon, we opened the box and began to sift through the notes. One stood out from the rest:

Don't fight over the butter. —Karen

This one begged for an explanation. Since Karen and her husband, Kevin, were our dear friends (and still are!), it was simple to get the story out of them.

One of the first and most volatile fights they ever had was over butter. Karen bought a new package of butter, but it turned out she didn't like the taste of it, so she threw it away. Kevin was irritated that Karen would be so wasteful, and Karen was irritated that he was trying to make her eat something she didn't want to eat. They went head-to-head over it, until he dug it out of the trash and put it back in the refrigerator. She refused to use it, so there it sat—a reminder of their huge fight.

Thankfully, they can both laugh about it now, and they agree the butter was not worth the fight. "Don't fight over the butter" has become a way for them to remember not to argue about little things that ultimately don't matter, which is what Karen wanted us to remember for our own marriage.

Another way to put it is the often-used phrase "Choose your battles," which is the basis of Dr. Richard Carlson's book *Don't Sweat the Small Stuff.* In it, he writes:

> *The truth is, life is rarely exactly the way we want it to be, and other people often don't act as we would like them to. Moment to moment, there are aspects of life that we like and others that we don't. There are always going to be people who disagree with you, people who do things differently, and things that don't work out. If you fight against this principle of life, you'll spend most of your life fighting battles.*

I don't know about you, but I have better things to do than to pick a fight over every little thing that doesn't go my way. Choosing your battles wisely seems simple enough when you're not in the middle of dealing with heated emotions. How can you know which battles are worth fighting and which ones to let go of? Maybe the next time you're about to lose your cool over the butter, you could ask yourself a few simple questions.

How to Choose Your Battles Wisely

How important is this to me?

This question alone can be enough to avoid a lot of unnecessary conflict. Choosing your battles is not about being taken advantage of and having your feelings stomped on. It's a matter of prioritizing, deciding which issues are worth your time and which simply are like boxing air—a waste of energy.

Can I bring this up in a way that doesn't make my spouse feel attacked?

You've asked yourself and decided this is worth bringing up. Now, instead of coming out with your dukes up, consider the best way to get your complaint heard. Most people don't respond well to being yelled at or criticized, so try a calmer approach. Maybe something like "I saw that brand-new package of butter in the garbage, and it really bugged me. Why did you throw it away?" Then, if you're Kevin, you'll need to decide if the wasted $2.69 is worth the peace you'll lose by fighting over it.

Now that we're fighting, is this worth it?

Sometimes you won't realize that a battle was not wisely chosen until you're already in the middle of it. Now that you're there, think about what you can do to end it well. It's possible that you don't think this issue is worth a fight but your spouse absolutely does. In that case, it's vital that you don't dismiss their feelings.

When Tony and I are in this situation, one of us might say, "Honey, I don't want to fight about the butter, but I do want to understand you better. Can we take a break?" Sometimes a break is all we need to gain some perspective.

Not everything is going to be worth fighting over. Constant nitpicking is divisive and unhealthy. The sooner we figure out which battles are worth fighting and which aren't, the more time we can spend in that joyful place we're all striving for in our marriages. Choose your battles wisely, and if you see a full package of butter in the garbage, maybe just leave it there.

For Discussion:

1   Do you have your own "fight over the butter" story? Share a time when you fought over something that you realized in the end wasn't worth it.

2   Read 1 Corinthians 9:24–27. Paul is talking about staying focused and not wasting his energy on things that aren't relevant to the race he's running. How do you think this relates to choosing our battles wisely in marriage?

3   Pray. Ask God to give you a spirit of unity so that you can more easily overlook the little irritations that might come up. Thank God for your marriage and for each other, and commit to continuing to develop an atmosphere of grace in your home.

Comparison Trap

> *For we would never dare to compare ourselves
> with people who have based their worth on self-
> commendation. They check themselves against and
> compare themselves with one another. It just shows
> that they don't have any sense!*
> —2 Corinthians 10:12

I love a night out with my girlfriends. I love catching up and laughing together. I especially love when my friends express adoration for their husbands. But every now and then, I admit, I'll hear a friend bragging about her husband and think, *My husband never does that.* If a friend's husband surprised her with a bouquet of flowers or a weekend getaway, of course I'm happy for her, but it's hard not to wish I had more of that in my marriage.

I wonder if my own husband ever feels that way. We're in a supper club with five other families, and all the wives in the group are fantastic at coming up with delicious meals. It's a running joke that all I can do is make spaghetti, order pizza, or cut fruit—that's my skill level. When I watch my husband truly enjoy a meal made by one of these women, I wonder if he wishes he had what their husbands have: a wife who likes to cook and is really good at it.

Whether we're comparing our spouses, our homes, our children, or ourselves, when we compare our lives to others', we're falling into a self-laid trap. Theodore Roosevelt is attributed with a saying that I wholeheartedly believe: "Comparison is the thief of joy." The danger in comparing is that we can begin to believe we're entitled to something we don't have. The Bible says that comparing ourselves to each other is foolish. It's a distraction; we get focused on each other instead of on God and all that he has done for us. We can't be both jealous and grateful at the same time.

Maybe you wish your husband were more handy around the house. Maybe you wish your wife were waiting for you at the end of the day with a hot and hearty meal made from scratch. Maybe you wish your husband of little words would write you poems to express his love. But since he's not Shakespeare the Handyman, and she's not the Pioneer Woman, you might be overlooking the gifts God has given you in your spouse. You might be dismissing who that person is and how they already love you.

When you find yourself with that twinge of jealousy, when you start to wish you had what you believe someone else has in their marriage, here are a few things you can do:

1   **Celebrate their joy!** One of the best ways out of the comparison trap is to get excited for other people and encourage them. Compliment your friend. Reinforce how loved she is by letting her know how wonderful it is that her husband surprises her with love notes around the

house. Hearing yourself say such complimentary things may just turn your own attitude from irritated to joyful.

2   **Play your own highlight reel.** Keep in mind that, most of the time, you're seeing only the "best-of clips" from your friends' life stories. This is especially true if you're comparing your real life to the lives you see on social media. Believe me, others' lives are not always as good as they appear. So instead of focusing on what they have that you don't, remember what you do have. Find something to brag about in your own partner. Remember when she picked up your favorite pint of ice cream just because? Or the other night when he offered to clean up after dinner and how loved you felt? Then go one step further and compliment your spouse verbally.

3   **Check yourself.** If you feel like your spouse may be lacking in some way, it's possible they're wishing for something more from you, too. So instead of comparing them to someone else, ask yourself if there are areas in which you can improve your own attitude and behavior. Maybe your wife wishes you'd give her an unsolicited back rub once in a while, no strings attached. Maybe your husband would love some company on his morning run, even though you'd rather stay in your warm bed a few minutes longer. Bring your best to your marriage, and you won't have time to think about someone else's.

Nobody's marriage is perfect all the time. Comparison will only ever serve to blind you from the goodness in your own life and, as the saying goes, steal your joy.

For Discussion:

1 Examine the accounts you're following on social media. Unfollow the accounts that consistently make you feel jealous, insecure, or unsatisfied with what you have. What we fill our minds with has a profound effect on how we feel about our own lives.

2 With your spouse, make a list of all of the things you love about your life. Take turns naming things you're grateful for.

3 Pray together, repent from any areas of jealousy and envy in your life, and thank God for the gift he's given you in each other.

Feed the Good Stuff

> *Finally, brothers and sisters, fill your minds with beauty and truth. Meditate on whatever is honorable, whatever is right, whatever is pure, whatever is lovely, whatever is good, whatever is virtuous and praiseworthy.*
> —*Philippians 4:8*

Feed the good stuff. Starve the bad stuff.

In marriage, we have to be purposeful about noticing, remembering, and appreciating the good stuff our partners bring into our lives. When we're in a regular practice of noticing the positive, it becomes easier to overlook and forgive the negative. The reason is that our brains work best with patterns. Your brain likes to connect similar thoughts into a story it can remember and apply to your life in general. When you focus on something positive, something you appreciate about your partner, your brain searches for more positive things to attach to that first thought.

Likewise, if you focus on something negative, your brain begins to bring up more negative thoughts to build that story. If I focus on something annoying that my husband does—like leaving hair clippings in the sink after he shaves—and let myself get irritated, the next thing I know I'm looking at his toothpaste splatters all over the mirror and the water all over the counter and his wet towel bunched up on the floor, and now I'm sure he's the dirtiest, most inconsiderate person ever. He's gross and I'm annoyed, and when he walks into the room, he'll be greeted by a wife who's ready to criticize him for things he didn't even know he did wrong.

This happens to all of us, but it doesn't have to. As famous relationship researcher Dr. John Gottman says in his book *The Seven Principles for Making Marriage Work*,

> *Fondness and admiration are two of the most crucial elements in a rewarding and long-lasting romance. Although happily married couples may feel driven to distraction at times by their partner's personality flaws, they still feel that the person they married is worthy of honor and respect. . . . If fondness and admiration are completely missing, reviving the relationship is impossible.*

Did you catch that? Without fondness and admiration, Gottman says, it's easy to lose honor and respect, without which your marriage doesn't stand a chance. He also acknowledges that it's natural to get irritated with each other. Can we honor and respect people we're always frustrated with? I don't think we can. So what can we do to keep our marriages strong even when we're irritated? We must practice feeding the good stuff. When you feed the good stuff, when you practice noticing and talking about the positive things, you automatically starve the bad stuff in your marriage. Focusing on good things makes it harder for your brain to hold onto the bad things.

Focusing on and feeding the good stuff is a habit—a discipline, a daily practice—that doesn't always come naturally. This is why I think Paul uses the Greek word *logizesthe*—translated as "meditate," "think about," or "fill your minds"—in the book of Philippians. Paul compels us to focus on positive thinking as if it's a choice, because in many ways, it is. Just because a negative or critical thought enters your mind, doesn't mean you should allow it to take over. If you practice, you can reflexively reject those criticisms by focusing on something good instead, enabling you to "put on your new self, modeled after the very likeness of God: truthful, righteous, and holy" (Ephesians 4:24).

Feeding the good stuff starves the bad stuff. Making a conscious effort to focus on the positive decreases your propensity to notice the negative. It's the little ways we speak and act toward each other every day that keep our marriages warm and inviting.

For Discussion:

1 Share with each other some of your favorite memories from when you were first dating. Notice how you feel about each other as you talk about your early days.

2 It's easy to get irritated about the little things that happen every day. Can you think of a positive way to look at, or talk about, something that bothered you recently?

3   Are you more prone to criticize aloud or stew about your criticisms silently? Does this idea of "feeding the good stuff" change that for you? If so, how?

4   Pray. Ask God to renew your mind and to help you focus on those things that are pure and lovely and good. Acknowledge the goodness God has put in your spouse and thank him for each other.

Love Is Not Like Chess

> *Be humble. Be gentle. Be patient.*
> *Tolerate one another in an atmosphere thick with love.*
> *Make every effort to preserve the unity the Spirit*
> *has already created, with peace binding you together.*
> *—Ephesians 4:2–3*

Before we were dating, Tony and I used to meet with some friends at a neighborhood bar called Piper's Creek. Piper's was a dimly lit pub with a few pool tables, some dartboards, and one bartender. The outer walls were lined with bookshelves and all sorts of old board games. Back then, though we weren't yet dating, we definitely *liked* each other. You know, "liked" in the kind of way that makes you try to say and do interesting, cool, and attractive things around each other.

One time, as we sat at one of the tables at Piper's, Tony asked if I'd like to play chess. "Sure," I said. "I'd love to!" I was embarrassingly enthusiastic, but who wouldn't want to play chess with someone they had a crush on? It's a game that takes a long time and involves only two players.

He pulled out the board and started to set up the pieces. I watched him and set my pieces up in the exact same way. He made his first move, and I thought it was a good one, so I made the exact same move. He made a few more moves, and each time I mirrored exactly what he did.

"You don't know how to play, do you?" he said.

"Well, I know the horse guy can take a left," I replied. "I know the pointy guy can go diagonal. And, yep, that's all I know about chess."

We laughed, and he started to teach me, but to this day I have no idea how to play chess, nor do I have any real desire to learn.

Tony and I still love playing games together, but if you're at a table playing with us, you'll quickly notice that we approach games very differently. I'm the type to play my hand, figure out my strategy at the start of the game, and move along at a relatively slow pace. Tony, on the other hand, is the card-counting, facial-expression-reading, block-your-next-move-just-because-he-can type of player. I play for fun, and he plays to win (which he claims is more fun).

Over the years, it's become clear that we approach just about everything in life differently, especially conflict. He likes to get it out on the table all at once. I like to wait until my thoughts are fully formed as reasonably as possible and be prepared for any contrary arguments before I broach an issue. In my mind, I'm being considerate by not lashing out at my husband. But sometimes, to Tony, it looks like I've shut him out.

Sometimes I want to play my frustrations out like a game of chess. I want to hold my anger and resentment close and watch to see if he'll figure out what he did wrong. Sometimes, when I'm hurt, I don't want to work with him on some sort of solution. I want, instead, to protect myself from him. I start thinking of him as an adversary and doing things for me instead of for us. But even as I'm playing all of this out in my mind, a conflicting phrase occurs to me over and over again: "We're on the same team. We're on the same team."

"Same team" is a phrase we use to remind ourselves that we're not married to an enemy whom we need to fight against. In a game where you're on the same team, you need to work together so that your team wins. If you play against your own team, you lose! In the case of marriage, we feel like we're not on the same team when we fail to listen to each other, and fail to really try to understand each other. If we do what comes naturally, just trying to be right and get our own way, we're playing the game as opponents. We need to, instead, come up with ways to listen and to try to understand each other, so that we can have a "same-team mind-set."

How about you? Are you and your spouse playing out your arguments as opponents, or are you attempting to be on the same team? Are you working hard to make your point, or are you working hard to have unity? Are you defending and protecting yourself, or are you defending and protecting your teammate and your marriage?

Once you get married, your role in the story of your life shifts entirely from being the star player to being a member of a team. The next time you go head-to-head with your partner, look him or her in the eye and remind each other that you're on the same team.

Think Like a Team

In marriage, we need to treat each other as teammates, not as opponents.

INDIVIDUAL/OPPONENT MIND-SET	SAME-TEAM MIND-SET
I am right, and I need to win this argument.	We need to understand each other better.
My spouse needs to parent the kids more like I do.	We want our kids to feel secure, which comes from us being consistent.
I'm putting my foot down on this one.	I feel strongly, but I'm willing to work on this until we can reach a solution.
I know this might be extravagant, but I deserve it, so I'm buying it.	I'll run big purchases by my spouse first to make sure we're on the same page. I'm willing to hear "No" or "Not right now."
"You never do anything around here!"	"Honey, I feel overwhelmed. Would you please help me with ____?"
Her tone is so disrespectful.	We're both feeling heated right now. I'll give her the benefit of the doubt. We could both probably use some time to cool down.
She needs to say she's sorry before I'll talk to her again.	Blaming isn't going to bring us any closer. The relationship is the most important thing.
Maybe I'll cool down, but he's not "getting any" tonight.	Withholding sex is manipulative and passive-aggressive. If I'm not ready to be intimate with him, I need to be honest about that.
This fight isn't going anywhere, but I won't be the one who gives in first.	This fight isn't going anywhere, so maybe I should attempt to make repairs.
We're so different. We'll never see eye to eye on this.	I don't see it the way he does right now, but I'm willing to let this one go, as I see he's passionate about it.

For Discussion:

1   Look at the "Think Like a Team" chart. What are the main differences you see between the individual/opponent mind-set and the same-team mind-set?

2   When it comes to fights and arguments, do you tend to want to get all your thoughts and feelings out at one time or to keep your thoughts to yourself for a while? What patterns have you noticed in your arguments?

3   In the book of Ephesians, Paul urges believers to be humble, gentle, and patient. How do you think this posture promotes unity?

4   Pray. Thank God for giving us a spirit of unity and ask him to show you where you have an individual/opponent mind-set. Ask God to give you peace and clarity as you pursue humility and patience with one another this week.

Laughter Is Not a Luxury

> Our mouths were filled with laughter; our tongues
> were spilling over into song.
> —Psalm 126:2

"What made you laugh today?" It's my favorite question to hear from my husband, Tony. It's his old standby way of moving the conversation from the usual stresses of life to something light. He wants me to tell him a story, and I know when he asks that he's really listening. Whether my answer has to do with something funny our girls did or a hilarious YouTube video, I know he wants me to share with him. And I know he wants to laugh, too!

If I'd made a list of "must-have" qualities in a man before I got married, "Must be able to make me laugh" would have been on it, but I don't think I could have told you why. It just seems fundamental. Now that we've been married for a little while, I realize that laughter is not a luxury that our marriage could survive without. We've gone through tough seasons without laughter, and those difficult times taught me that laughter is essential.

As a teenager, I was diagnosed with dysthymia, a type of mild depression that sits always beneath the surface of my life. While I can function without medication and live a mostly normal life, it's far too easy for me to slip into seasons of deep, dark clinical depression, where medication becomes my lifeline and laughter seems impossible. And when my spirit is crushed, it crushes our whole family. As isolated as depression can make me feel, its effects are felt by everyone I love. Knowing that darkness, however, has given me an appreciation for the immense blessings of true joy and laughter.

As Proverbs 17:22 says, "A joy-filled heart is curative balm, but a broken spirit hurts all the way to the bone." So Tony and I find simple ways to make each other laugh. Laughter connects us. It helps us relax by releasing endorphins, biological chemicals known to relieve pain and stress. It's more than a figurative "curative balm"—laughter truly is good medicine.

Laughing together is also an access point for intimacy. When people laugh together, they're likely to talk more, touch more, and make eye contact more frequently. Knowing I can make my husband laugh with the right turn of phrase or a simple silly face is a sign that we have a connection with each other that we don't have with anyone else. We understand each other in a way that nobody else has access to. When we're laughing, we're able to let our guards down and be more open with each other. And if he makes a joke and I don't laugh, it's a clear signal there's a disconnect between us, which means we've got to bridge that gap, uproot whatever is lying beneath the surface preventing our joy, work through it, and laugh again.

Laughter is also a way to celebrate, like in Psalm 126:1–2: "Remember when the Eternal brought back the exiles to Zion? It was as if we were dreaming—Our mouths were filled with laughter; our tongues were spilling over into song." When God brings us through a difficult season, whether it's depression, grief, or any other kind of struggle, being able to come through to the other side and laugh again is a sign that our perspective is on him and our joy is complete.

Once you realize the blessings in laughter, you'll begin craving and looking for opportunities to laugh. Whether we're watching the latest Brian Regan comedy special, playing dress-up games with our girls, or sharing funny "remember when" stories with each other, everything about our relationship feels better when we can laugh.

For Discussion:

1   Share with each other about something that made you laugh today.

2   Share your funniest memory of each other.

3   How can you see laughter as a sign of celebration in your own life? What hardships have you been through that you can now look back on and smile?

4   Pray. Thank God for making us multidimensional beings who can laugh. Thank him that each person's laughter is unique to them, and that when we laugh together, we build a chorus of joy. Pray for the awareness to notice more joyful moments throughout the week.

Walk with the Wise

People seldom improve when they have no other model but themselves to copy.
—Oliver Goldsmith

We were so taken by you that we not only eagerly shared with you God's good news, but we also shared with you our own lives. That's how much you've come to mean to us.
—1 Thessalonians 2:8

Nobody becomes an expert on their own. Everyone, from NFL players to professional chefs, can give you several examples of people who inspired them—people who modeled what was possible. The most successful professionals in any field will tell you who their mentor is without skipping a beat. Married people need mentors, too. If we're going to succeed, we need real-life examples to see how it's done.

With just six weeks until our wedding, Tony and I became premarital-counseling dropouts. It's not that we thought we had it all figured out; we just could no longer afford the $100 per hour that it was costing us. Still, we wanted some coaching, so after the wedding, we came up with another idea: We decided to find another couple to mentor us.

After talking it through, we zeroed in on a couple from our church: Rich and Barbara. We didn't know much about them, but they seemed joyful, they volunteered with kids at church, and their own kids were sweet and fun to be around. We judged a tree by its fruit, and hoped our lives would bear similar fruit after we'd been married as long as they had. It turned out to be one of the best decisions we've made to date!

Tony and I were married only a few months when we started on this journey with Rich and Barbara. The four of us agreed that meeting twice a month was plenty for all of our busy schedules. They chose a book for us to work through as a way of springboarding discussion topics, and away we went. We alternated between our home and theirs and took turns making dinner for each other. Once we finished the book, we had a celebratory dinner in downtown Seattle. By that time, we had been so raw and honest with one another that we knew we had close friends for life.

Proverbs 13:20 tells us, "One who walks with the wise becomes wise." Do you have wise married people in your life? Do you make an effort to spend time with them? Finding and building a relationship with your own marriage mentors might be your next step. Here are four actions to help you on your way:

1 **Judge the tree by its fruit.** Jesus said, "No good tree bears bad fruit, and no bad tree bears good fruit. You can know a tree by the fruit it bears. You don't find figs on a thorn bush, and you can't pick grapes from a briar bush. It's the same with people" (Luke 6:43–45). Look for people who are producing

the kind of fruit you want to produce from your marriage. Find a couple who is joyful, generous, kind to each other, and fun, if that's what you want your marriage to look like.

2   **Do a little digging.** If you don't already know the answers, ask a couple these questions: How long have you been married? How old are your kids? What's one of your favorite things to do together? The first question is the most important. Tony and I wanted to be mentored by a couple who had been married at least 20 years. We have a long-term vision for our marriage and wanted to be around people who had been standing together through a significant amount of time. The next couple of questions were a little less significant, but they helped us get to know Rich and Barbara a bit before making the big ask.

3   **Once you've identified a couple you hope will mentor you, ask them!** It might be intimidating, but do it anyway. Tony and I made sure we asked as specifically and casually as we could. (In other words, Tony made me do it.) I think asking in person is better than over e-mail, Facebook, or text message, but however you ask, make it personal.

4   **Make a plan.** Find a format that works for both couples. Make sure to have a start and end to your timeline so that you all know you're not committing to something for the rest of your lives. Honor each other's families and other time commitments, leaving room to reschedule and change locations when you need to.

Developing a mentoring relationship may not feel natural at first. It's easy to believe the lie that we should be able to figure this marriage stuff out on our own. If you've never been mentored yourself, professionally or otherwise, it might feel a little silly to ask someone to speak into your life in this way. But don't let that feeling rob you of building key relationships with people who are a little further along in their marriage than you are. Wise people with healthy relationships didn't get that way by living life in a silo away from the influence of those around them. Furthermore, they may be eager to share the joy they've found in their marriage with you.

For Discussion:

1   Talk with your spouse about couples who inspire you. It doesn't matter if they've been married longer than you or not; just think through and name the characteristics of their marriage that you admire.

2   Can you think of couples who have been married at least five years longer than you whom you enjoy being around? Make a list if more than one couple comes to mind.

3   Talk about the four steps. Are you ready to reach out to another couple to mentor you? Think this through and make a plan together.

4   Pray. Thank God for the wisdom he gives and ask him to open your hearts to a mentoring relationship. Ask God to bring a couple to mind if you can't think of anyone and to help you follow through with your plan to seek out marriage mentors. Pray that he will cover that relationship with grace and wisdom, and that your request for mentorship be a blessing and not a burden to anyone.

In Sickness and in Health

> *After washing their feet and picking up His garments,*
> *[Jesus] reclined at the table again.*
> *"Do you understand what I have done to you? You*
> *call Me Teacher and Lord, and truly, that is who I am.*
> *So if your Lord and Teacher washes your feet, then*
> *you should wash one another's feet. I am your*
> *example; keep doing what I do."*
> *—John 13:12–15*

Recently, my family was hit hard in the winter months with one kind of virus or another. We missed out on a lot. It wasn't fun. For the most part, I stayed relatively symptom-free while I watched my girls and my husband suffer. I was glad not to be sick, but a part of me wished I could be the one who got babied and coddled, instead of being the one who was constantly checking temperatures and serving chicken soup. Caring for sick people is exhausting! The toddler in me wanted to stomp my foot and declare, "It's not fair!" I had plenty of time to think while I cradled my feverish darlings, and during that time, the words from my wedding vows called to me: "In sickness and in health."

I used to think that classic line applied to romantic faithfulness in the face of some serious illness like cancer or Alzheimer's disease. I pictured holding hands on the side of a hospital bed and reading to my dear husband as he moaned in and out of consciousness. I did not picture making sure our medicine cabinet was stocked with anti-diarrhea pills and catching vomit in my hands.

Of course, the roles have been reversed. About three months after our wedding, I came down with one of the worst stomach viruses I've ever experienced. I can hardly remember a time when I felt more disgusting or helpless. As a new wife, I was also mortified for my husband to see me that way. Tony graciously ran me a bath, cleaned up after me (I'll spare you the details), and kept any disgust he may have been feeling completely hidden from me. At that point, I knew the honeymoon phase was over and we were really married. He had seen me at my worst and still put my needs before his own.

Since then, we have traded turns caretaking a number of times. He's been a witness to the birth of all three of his daughters. And yes, birth is a miracle, but it's a really gross miracle, and recovering from it isn't pleasant. But the truth is, the illnesses and health setbacks we've experienced are minor compared to any we may face as we truly age. The reality is that as a person moves from the role of partner to the role of caregiver, an incredible amount of stress can be added to the relationship.

Taking care of someone who is sick, whether it is a cold or something more serious and chronic, is a true test of selflessness and love. But the burden doesn't have to be carried by the married couple alone. In a community, we share each other's burdens. Those people who watched you get married weren't present simply to be an audience to your grand show; the idea is that they stand by you and you by them. Those guests are meant to be your support system, believing so much in your union that they're willing to make sacrifices themselves to see it sustained.

Tony and I have had a few opportunities to care for our friends in practical ways by sitting next to a hospital bed or delivering a meal. And more times than we can count, we have received care from our community. I've had friends not only drop off meals when my kids were sick, but also offer to care for my kids when I've been sick, and even come to my house to fold my laundry. This is the beauty of being a part of a local church or community: You invest yourself in others and, in turn, they invest themselves in you.

Still, once my gracious friends leave, I'm faced with my one and only in the moments I don't feel so attractive or romantic. Dealing with the stress of illness can be a turning point in the life of a marriage. We all have the opportunity in that moment to either fend for ourselves or to put someone else's needs above our own. Psychologists like Thomas Bradbury, codirector of the Relationship Institute at UCLA, have studied these defining moments. Reporting on Bradbury's findings, Stuart Wolpert writes:

> The couples that were willing to make sacrifices
> within their relationships were more effective in
> solving their problems. . . . "It's a robust finding,"
> Bradbury said. "[This] kind of commitment predicted

lower divorce rates and slower rates of deterioration in the relationship."

Of the 172 married couples in the study, 78.5 percent were still married after 11 years, and 21.5 percent were divorced. The couples in which both people were willing to make sacrifices for the sake of the marriage were significantly more likely to have lasting and happy marriages.

A willingness to sacrifice is key. The resolve to walk into situations where you can only serve your partner without expecting anything in return is the kind of commitment that will see a relationship through all of life's ups and downs. A lot of marriage is deciding to put someone else's needs above our own. In setting aside our comfort and serving those we love, we demonstrate the servant heart of Jesus to each other.

For Discussion:

1 Were the words "in sickness and in health" a part of your wedding vows? If so, what did you imagine they meant when you said them? If not, how did you promise to care for one another?

2 How was illness handled when you were a child? How do you think that impacts how you navigate illness with each other now?

3   Do you have people in your lives who have recently had a
    baby or are currently dealing with illness? Make a plan to
    take them a meal or offer to serve them in some other
    practical way.

4   Pray. Thank God that he is our healer. Ask him to develop
    in you a servant's heart to sacrifice for one another and
    lovingly serve each other as illnesses come and go in
    your lives.

Holding Hands

So I give you a new command: Love each other
deeply and fully. Remember the ways that I have
loved you, and demonstrate your love for others
in those same ways. Everyone will know you as My
followers if you demonstrate your love to others.
—John 13:34–35

I'm not tall—some might even say that at 5 feet 3½ inches, I'm short—so I get anxious in crowds. As a teenager, I got used to being squished and stomped on whenever I went out to see live music, and I still feel my chest tighten and my shoulders clench when I have to go into a crowd. My husband, Tony, on the other hand, isn't bothered at all. He's 6 feet 2 inches and walks confidently through crowds, weaving his way in the direction he wants to go. When we're together, he grabs my hand and I follow. As he leads me, I know I'm safe, and my anxiety level goes way down.

Moving through a crowd is not the only time he holds my hand. In fact, he holds my hand most of the time when we're out together. One day, we picked up a friend of his whose car had broken down. The three of us stopped at a grocery store on our way to take him home. We all walked in together, and naturally, Tony held my hand. "Whoa, PDA!" his friend said. "Don't let my wife see you. I never hold her hand in public."

Truthfully, until his friend made such a big deal about it, we didn't even know it was a thing. Tony told him he was an idiot and then wrapped his arm tightly around my shoulder just to make a point. Showing me affection publicly—holding my hand, kissing my cheek, putting his arms around me—was not remotely embarrassing to him. It's something about our relationship I've probably taken for granted. He has never been stingy with his affection. He's never made me feel strange for leaning into him or squeezing him in a tight hug for a few extra seconds.

We aren't affectionate for anyone else's benefit but our own. And yet, as we demonstrate our love in these little physical ways, we point to a bigger love: God's love. God's love isn't stingy or embarrassed, and he never withholds it from us. God pours out his big love generously, not just in Christ's sacrifice on the cross, but daily and moment by moment. And when we're so full with God's love, loving each other comes naturally.

During the birth of our third daughter, I needed my husband's physical presence in the most crucial way. I was struggling through painful contractions. There were times I felt weak, inadequate, and even scared. Tony held my hand and never let go. Between contractions, I was able to look at him, and I just marveled. I had been gripping him so hard, pulling down on him by the shoulders with all of my strength. No doubt he had war wounds from the frenzy of a shockingly fast delivery. Still, he held my hand, cheered me on, and gave me strength. At the end, once our daughter was born, he held my hand again as he prayed over our newborn and me. There's a saying attributed to the ancient philosopher Lao Tzu: "Being deeply loved by someone gives you strength, while loving someone deeply gives you courage." Strength and courage were just what I needed, and loving and being loved by Tony gave me both.

Holding hands is a simple act of affection, and yet it can carry such profound meaning. According to *Psychology Today*, research shows that holding hands and other forms of physical affection add to feelings of security and attachment and reduce the stress hormones in the brain. Holding your partner's hand when they're describing a stressful situation can help them feel calm or even lower the intensity of a fight.

There is immense power in this simple act. It takes only a moment and a little bit of good intention to reach for the one you love. I hope you give and receive the benefits of holding hands as often as possible, practice affection, and lean into that big love that God pours out over your marriage.

For Discussion:

1 Would you say you hold hands most of the time or hardly ever? What does each of you think about hand-holding?
2 What are other small physical ways you enjoy sharing affection?
3 Hold hands and share with each other what you would like to pray about. Then pray while holding hands.

Slow to Anger

> *Whoever is patient and slow to anger shows great*
> *understanding, but whoever has a quick temper*
> *magnifies his foolishness.*
> *—Proverbs 14:29*

I'll never forget my first fight with Tony. Okay, that's not completely true. Other than a lot of yelling, I barely remember it at all. What I do remember is how I felt. We'd been dating only a few months, and I was madly in love. As we argued and yelled at each other in his Bronco, I remember feeling so shocked and hurt that we were actually fighting. I didn't hear a word he said. I'm sure he wasn't hearing me. I kept thinking, *Is this how he fought in his last relationship? I hate this!*

Tony dated his previous girlfriend for 10 years. Yes, you read that correctly. They got together when they were just 16 years old and stayed together until they were 26. Most people, including their families (and me!), thought they would get married. During those 10 years, I assumed they had developed their routines, their own expectations of one another, and their own way of fighting.

I thought about that as we unleashed on each other that night. I also thought about my own three-year, on-again-off-again relationship pre-Tony, and the habits of fighting I'd had with my own ex-boyfriend.

I didn't want to fight with Tony. Even more, I was sure I didn't want to fight like this. I didn't want us to treat each other the way we had treated our exes. I wanted something new, something healthy with this man I was falling in love with. We calmed down eventually, held each other, and agreed that fighting was awful. No matter how much insight the experience gave me, I didn't want to repeat it. We kissed and agreed on just one thing: no yelling.

It turns out that yelling just doesn't work. Though it may make your voice significantly louder, yelling does not actually help your partner hear you. In fact, it does the opposite. When you yell, the brain of the person you're yelling at senses danger and begins to spend its energy assessing how to deal with the perceived threat. The well-known fight-or-flight response system kicks in, causing your spouse to become defensive and yell back (fight mode) or withdraw and stonewall (flight mode). In either case, they certainly aren't listening to you. Whatever you yelled—however important it may be to you, however passionately you feel—is now completely lost on them. They see red, they hear loud sirens, and they react. They do not see the person they love reaching out to be understood.

Yelling at someone isn't usually the most thought-out response to a situation. When we yell, it's usually because we've lost control over ourselves. But the Bible exhorts us to learn to control our reactions, to slow down, and to respond to offenses with patience and grace. And God promises that as we submit ourselves to the character-refining work of the Holy Spirit, he will give us the ability to do this well.

Fighting and arguing are perfectly healthy and natural parts of marriage—even happy marriages. Still, if you can remember that you're on the same team with your spouse, if you can take a breath and remember to keep the volume low, the fights you do have can be productive and insightful instead of divisive. Be patient with one another and slow down your response time when you start to feel angry.

10 Rules for Fair Fighting

1 No name-calling.

2 No Interrupting.

3 No blaming or accusations.

4 No cursing.

5 No yelling.

6 No sarcasm.

7 No defensiveness.

8 No generalizations ("you always" or "you never").

9 No physical/emotional intimidating gestures/ violence/threats.

10 No walking out without naming a follow-up time.

For Discussion:

1. Look at the 10 rules for fair fighting. Which of these rules are you most likely to break in your fights with your spouse?

2. How do you think agreeing to a set of rules could help your arguments be more productive?

3. Proverbs 14:29 says whoever has a quick temper magnifies his foolishness. What do you think this means?

4. Pray. Ask God to be with you in the midst of your arguments. Ask the Holy Spirit to refine your temper and increase your patience with yourselves and with each other. Ask each other for forgiveness for the times you have lost your tempers and raised your voices, and commit to approaching each other with kindness and respect.

Cast Your Cares

*Cast your troubles upon the Eternal; His care
is unceasing! He will not allow His righteous to
be shaken.*
—Psalm 55:22

Some say that anxiety is when a person is consumed with the
future and depression is when they are consumed with the past.
Staying in the present might be the cure for both, but that can
be hard to do. When I get stressed, for example, my first instinct
is never to pray or even talk it out. Instead, I pull inward, and my
thoughts begin to spiral. What might have been just one simple
task added to my day can send me down a horrid trail of panic
about all the other things I need to get done, all the kids' schedules, what we need from Costco, and somebody's birthday is
coming up, and I really need to get back in a writing routine, and
gosh, I'm out of shape, and nobody has clean pajamas, and ahhh!

When my mind is in this state, it's a risky move to approach
me. I'm so in my head with all the items on my mental to-do list
that if anyone tries to talk to me, I feel like they're purposely
intruding on my thoughts. I snap! Then I feel bad and apologize

and turn inward all over again. It's not fun for me or anyone close to me.

But I have found one trick that helps me breathe and settles my heart: I make a list.

Now, I'm a natural list-maker. I don't start a day of work without one. I have lists upon lists in my phone for everything from groceries to dream guests for my podcast. But the kind of list that really helps my anxiety is the one I write and then e-mail to my husband that starts like this:

> *Subject: All of the things on my plate that are not getting done right now . . .*
>
> *Hey Tony,*
>
> *I'm feeling stressed and overwhelmed, and I realized I have a ton of stuff on my mind. I keep thinking I'll get to these things, so I haven't mentioned them to you. But I can't do this by myself. I need your help. Here's my list . . .*

Exhale.

As soon as I hit send on that e-mail, I feel tons better, even before he's responded. There's something powerful in simply writing out and naming the things that are weighing us down. There's a release. I feel my shoulders soften and my brow unfurrow, and I realize I've been carrying these burdens not just in my mind but also on my face and in my body.

And you know what? Tony *wants* to know what's on my mind. He wants to carry my burdens along with me. When we carry our burdens together, the load is lighter. The Apostle Paul tells us, "Love bears all things, believes all things, hopes all things, endures all things" (1 Corinthians 13:7, ESV). Being a team in marriage isn't just about the equitable division of responsibilities, it's about sharing our secret burdens, becoming one in mind and spirit. When I withhold from him the things that are on my mind, I put a little wedge between us. I may think I'm doing him a favor by keeping the stress to myself, but that's a lie filled with pride. In truth, we need to practice being open with one another even about the seemingly insignificant details.

Tony usually responds to an e-mail like that by telling me which of the items he's going to help with or which we can skip altogether. He's on my team, and he wants to work through solutions together. He's not offended by my burdens; he's thankful to be the one to carry them with me. He's thankful he can bring them up in prayer alongside me.

Practicing this burden sharing with each other is also a way to access the burden-lightening power of prayer and trust in Jesus. In the Psalms, we're invited to cast our burdens onto God. When I'm stressed, I sometimes forget that I'm actually not alone—I have a redeemer who welcomes me to share my stress with him. My husband is my real-life personal illustration that sharing my burdens is a way to stay connected. Because I keep that in mind when I take my list to the Lord, I deepen my spiritual connection and my heart goes from anxious to peaceful. And just like sending that e-mail, the peace doesn't come because all my to-dos are mystically marked as "done" through prayer. The peace comes because I've brought my list to the Prince of Peace, whose spirit invades my soul and changes my perspective. "I've got this," he says. "You're not alone. That's what I'm here for."

For Discussion:

1   Take a few minutes to make a list of all the things that are on your mind, responsibilities that need to get taken care of, and anything causing you stress or anxiety.
2   Share your lists with each other, and see if there are areas where you can offer to help.
3   Pray. Bring your burdens to the Prince of Peace and ask him for clarity and perspective. Ask for unity so that you can work through your stresses as a team instead of striving individually.

Pay Attention

> *My bride, you are a fountain in a garden,*
> *a well of life-giving water flowing down*
> *from Lebanon.*
> *—Song of Solomon 4:15*

I consider myself very lucky to have married a man who loves to cook. Tony puts a lot of thought into what he makes, and as a perfectionist, he's always trying to make each dish turn out better than the last. It can be thrilling when he makes something for the first time—he's excited and wants to get it exactly right.

One Tuesday, he came home from work with all the ingredients to make chicken piccata. He served it over creamy mashed potatoes with perfectly prepared asparagus. With a glass of pinot grigio, I was in heaven with every bite.

"Seriously, Babe, this is incredible!" I told him. "What inspired you to make this tonight?"

"Well, I was at work today and they had chicken piccata as a special in the café. I thought, *If Honey were here, that's what she'd get*, so I ordered it. It was okay, but I was sure I could make it better if I tried. I figured, since it's one of your favorite dishes to eat at a restaurant, I should learn to make it for you myself."

I sat stunned that he was so silently perceptive about the things I enjoy. I do order chicken piccata a lot, but if someone asked me my favorite food, it probably wouldn't have immediately come to mind. It was like he knew me better than I knew myself. On top of that, it made me feel so loved to know that he thought of me at work, looked up recipes, went to the grocery store on a mission, and was meticulous about making this meal perfect. And he didn't wait for some special occasion to blow me away with his creation; he just went the extra mile on an otherwise ordinary Tuesday night at home, simply because he knows me and he loves me and it motivates him to do things like figure out how to make something I would enjoy.

One of the core longings of all human beings is to be known. We were created for the purpose of relationships, that we would experience connection and pleasure. There is something inside each of us that yearns for others to really understand us. Paying attention, truly studying for the sake of understanding someone else, is one of the greatest ways you can express love. Do I always feel loved when he makes dinner? Absolutely! Did I feel extra loved once I understood the motivation behind this particular dinner? You bet!

Whether you're just starting out in your relationship or you've been married for decades, there is always more to discover about the person you love. It is precisely this kind of knowing that keeps couples together for the long journey of marriage.

For Discussion:

1   Read Song of Solomon 7:1–9. Notice the details the speaker uses to describe his love. What is he paying attention to?

2   Now take turns describing at least five characteristics that you love and admire about each other. Describe them as if you were describing your partner to someone who has never met them.

3   Is there anything your partner said in response to question two that surprised you? In what ways are they paying attention that you didn't realize?

4   Pray. Ask God to open your eyes to one another in new ways. Thank him for the gift that your partner is to you, and for the specific things you love about your partner. Ask God to cover your love so that nothing comes between you.

Get Beyond Yourselves

Don't let selfishness and prideful agendas take over.
Embrace true humility, and lift your heads to extend
love to others. Get beyond yourselves and protect-
ing your own interests; be sincere, and secure your
neighbors' interests first.
—Philippians 2: 3–4

"Gotta do the gottas before you do the wannas." It's one of many mantras in our home. I wish I'd thought of it, but it's actually a phrase Tony heard from his parents growing up. He shared it with me once—along with his disdain for it. But I loved it so much that I started using it with our kids. If they ask for time with their electronics or to watch a show on Netflix, I usually say, "Sure." Then I look around and add, "How does your room look? Are the toys picked up in the living room? Ya gotta do the gottas before you do the wannas. As soon as everything is taken care of, you can definitely watch a show."

As adults, we're bombarded with the "gottas" every single day. You've got to go to work. You've got to do the laundry. You've got to pay your bills. You've got to go to that very long meeting that feels like a big waste of time. You've got to remember to take the garbage out to the curb. The gottas are the part of adulthood that you couldn't imagine when you were a kid and all you wanted was to grow up and do everything by yourself. Well, we're grown-ups now, and we have a lot of things to do.

Because there are so many gottas, it's pretty easy to overlook the "wannas" and what I call the "get-tos." I get to eat whatever I want (not that I should). I get to snuggle my kids. I get to stay up late. I get to listen to music I like throughout the day. The get-tos are the opportunities we have to enjoy life every day if we'll only look for them.

In fact, you'll have an opportunity to go out of your way to be kind to your spouse today. I promise. You could bring them an unexpected latte. You could text them a sweet "thinking of you" message. You could check in with them to see if there's anything they need from the store on your way home. You could change their windshield wipers. You could rub their shoulders.

In marriage, it's easy to end up in our own lanes, running parallel to each other. Often, we're so consumed with our usual responsibilities that we forget to connect with each other outside of making sure all our gottas are taken care of. We can find ourselves waiting for our partners to extend kindness and generosity to us, forgetting that we should initiate kindness ourselves. When we decide to be purposeful about it and look for ways to make their day better, the blessing doubles. When we joyfully serve each other, our perspective rises off of ourselves and our gottas, and our hearts expand, allowing more love to flow through.

We need to be deliberate about looking for little ways to add joy, finding points of intersection and connection, to meet each other there, so we continue to grow together. If we don't prioritize those points of connection, we become exactly what we don't want to be: roommates.

Today, you and I *get to* figure out a way to show and tell the most important people in our lives, our spouses, that we love them. It's not a gotta, it's a get-to. Don't let the opportunity slip by you.

For Discussion:

1   What were some responsibilities you had growing up that you really didn't like?
2   What is one thing you love about being an adult?
3   Share a memory of when you were delighted by something your partner did for you.
4   Pray. Thank God for the many little ways he blesses you each day. Ask him to open your hearts and eyes to ways you can show kindness and humility to each other.

Marriage Is a Sanctuary

> *Now all of us, with our faces unveiled, reflect the*
> *glory of the Lord as if we are mirrors; and so we are*
> *being transformed, metamorphosed, into His same*
> *image from one radiance of glory to another, just as*
> *the Spirit of the Lord accomplishes it.*
> —2 Corinthians 3:18

I thought my marriage would be a relationship with this man whom I fell in love with. I thought we'd hang out and make out and see what became of our lives together. Instead, my marriage has become a sanctuary. Marriage is a holy place, and nothing holy can be experienced without transformation.

One day after a busy morning, I caught myself in a mirror and noticed that my eyeliner had been smudged under my right eye for who knows how long. Now that I saw it in the mirror, I could wipe it away and fix my face. But I couldn't do anything about the way everyone else saw me all morning. They didn't tell me.

I didn't know. It was too late to try to go back and fix it. I just had to move on.

This marriage, this sanctuary that I live in every single day, has mirrors on every surface. To live here in this sanctuary is to come face-to-face with my least flattering angles. Because, unlike any other relationship I've ever had, I can't hide in this one. I'm here and he's here, and even though it's not his intention to point out all of my mistakes and messiness, when I'm here with him, I can't help but see it all myself.

This sanctuary is not safe if I think of "safe" meaning the same as "comfortable." In this sanctuary, I'm challenged by these mirrors that show me who I really am at times: selfish, cynical, and self-righteous. When I see those smudges, I am forced to either dig in my heels or change. Change is uncomfortable. And yet, in this sanctuary, I can experience change and be transformed into the woman I actually want to become—generous, optimistic, and humble. I am partnered with a man who sees me and sees what we can be together: people transformed by God's love. We love each other in a way that causes love to overflow and wipe the smudges away so that we can shine the way we were meant to.

This sanctuary, this character-refining relationship, this daily thing we're both up to our necks in: this is the place where I believe we experience God. He's here in the dailies, calling out to us that our relationship with him should be as daily and life-long as our marriage. That we would see him ever-present in our day-to-day and connect with him in the gritty reality of life, until eventually, we look back on all the days we've been here in this mirror-filled sanctuary and see that we've done some good work together, and that we built this life on love.

When people say that marriage is hard work, it sounds like they're saying it's hard to live with someone else. That's true sometimes, but I think it's much harder to live in ignorance of our true selves. Of course, marriage isn't the only way to understand yourself, but most of us don't realize how very selfish we are until we're around someone for whom we must sacrifice. We don't see the way our deep darkness impacts our relationships until someone else's light shows up daily to expose it. We don't see our self-righteousness until we're faced with the option to either be right or be in a relationship. We spend most of our lives around people who won't gently hold up a mirror in front of us or require us to face our own dirt. We're all so polite that we don't dare take our own thumbs and wipe the smudges from one another's faces. The hard work of marriage is facing ourselves and deciding we are ready to grow, ready to let go of all the ways we knew to live and discover a new way to be in partnership with someone else.

It's in this sanctuary, in this partnership, that we learn what it means to humbly admit that we were wrong and ask for forgiveness. It is here that we learn to forgive. It is here that we learn to serve someone other than ourselves, and to put someone else's joy ahead of our own. It is here that we learn patience and kindness as sacrificial acts of love. We learn to temper our bad attitudes or pay the price of unnecessary strife. We learn that not every battle is worth fighting. Because even though Jesus taught us to turn the other cheek, even though he said the last shall be first and the first shall be last, even though he showed us that to love is to literally lay your life down, no other relationship gives us so many daily opportunities to practice this the way marriage does.

Some people may not need marriage to learn those lessons. For the rest of us, God provides a partner. He gives us a battle buddy, an *ezer kenegdo* (see Week 6), and a daily and forever friend with whom we can stand shoulder to shoulder and eye to eye and say, "Let's do this together. Let's try."

For Discussion:

1   What, if anything, have you learned about yourself since being married? How was this revealed to you?
2   In what ways do you see God using your marriage to refine your character?
3   Pray. Ask God in his mercy to hold those mirrors up for you. Pray for the humility to honestly face what you see and the courage to make steps to allow him to refine your character.

Week 20

Sabbath

> *Come to Me, all who are weary and burdened,*
> *and I will give you rest.*
> —Matthew 11:28

We like to keep busy. Our calendars are maxed out. *MarketWatch* reports that 51 percent of people who are offered paid vacation time don't take all of it. Are you a part of that 51 percent? Busyness is a detriment to a healthy marriage because it leaves us less room to connect with each other. And busyness has never been a characteristic that God is trying to cultivate within us. When God first gave Moses the Ten Commandments, he said, "You and your family are to remember the Sabbath Day; set it apart and keep it holy" (Exodus 20:8). Taking a full day off, it seems, was one of God's top 10 priorities for his people. It was so important, in fact, that people could be (and were) executed if they didn't.

You could think of the Sabbath as God asking for one-seventh, or about 14 percent, of his people's time. Even more than the tithe, which requires setting aside only 10 percent of one's earnings for God, the Sabbath lets people demonstrate that they trust in God to provide for their needs. He asked them for 24 of the 168 hours they have in a week, sundown to sundown, on just one day. Would they trust him enough to give him their time, to understand that if they rested in him, they'd still have their needs met?

Now, we know that keeping the Sabbath holy was introduced in the Old Testament, but the New Testament has important things to teach us about the Sabbath as well. After Jesus was accused of breaking the Sabbath by feeding hungry people, he said, "The Sabbath was made for the needs of human beings, and not the other way around" (Mark 2:27). What he meant was that the Sabbath was instituted for the good of humankind, for rest from our work and rest from our worries and anxieties.

This rest, this Sabbath, is less a matter of a certain day and more a matter of a certain person: Jesus. Jesus himself is the Sabbath. "Come to Me, all who are weary and burdened, and I will give you rest. Put My yoke upon your shoulders—it might appear heavy at first, but . . . My yoke is easy, and My burden is light" (Matthew 11:28–30). He's the one offering us rest, inviting us to be with him, reminding us that if we'll come be still with him, he'll meet us there every single time. The Bible extends this invitation to us over and over again:

Listen! The Lord, the Eternal, the Holy One of Israel says,
Eternal One: *In returning and rest, you will be saved.*
In quietness and trust you will find strength.
—Isaiah 30:15

The Lord will fight for you; you need only to be still.
—Exodus 14:14 (ESV)

Be still, and know that I am God.
—Psalm 46:10 (ESV)

Over and over again, God asks us to slow down, to be still, to rest. In God's pursuit of our heart, his constant invitations to stillness are like the words of a neglected lover pleading with us for more time and more connection. He calls us to rest, and in resting, we reset our priorities. Are our daily tasks really more important than our relationships? Busyness is a manifestation of misplaced priorities. Busyness leads to disconnection. Thriving relationships require our time, not just our intentions, and this is especially true in marriage. In order to truly connect with each other and grow together, we must dedicate our most precious resource—our time—to that which matters most. God calls us to rest, not for his sake, but for ours.

For Discussion:

1   What do your days off together look like?
2   Look at your calendar. Based on what you see, would you say that you have prioritized busyness or rest and time together?
3   How have you seen this dance between restfulness and busyness affect your relationship with each other?
4   Pray. Thank God that his presence in your life brings rest. Ask him to bring a spirit of restfulness and reflection into your marriage so that you can deepen your connection with one another.

Ask for What You Need

> *You do not have because you have chosen not to ask.*
> —James 4:2

Tony noticed how I was struggling to get out of the house on my own after the birth of our first daughter, Claire, so he encouraged me to join a women's Bible study. Before the first meeting, I was a ball of nerves. Would Tony and Claire be okay without me? Would I be too awkward with these new women? Tony assured me everything would be fine and nearly pushed me out the front door.

He was right. It was more than fine. I enjoyed my time and felt refreshed. I smiled the entire drive home, eager to thank Tony for insisting I go and excited to tell him how it went. But as I walked in the door of our little apartment, the first thing I saw was a sink full of dirty dishes and baby bottles. Tony was in the living room playing video games, the baby already asleep in her room. I went instantly from refreshed to frustrated.

I dropped my bag on the floor, took off my coat, rolled up my sleeves, and got to work. Tony paused his game and asked, "How was it? Did you have fun?"

"It was great," I replied with a straight face, my hands deep in the sink. I never did thank him; I just finished the dishes and went to bed.

The next week was a replay of the first. The third week, as I was getting ready to go, I realized that now I was anticipating coming home and being annoyed. Then it hit me: What if Tony didn't know I wanted his help with the kitchen? What if, after a rough evening with the baby, he just wanted to sit down and relax with his video games? What if he wasn't leaving the sink full of dishes and bottles just to bug me?

James 4:1–2 says, "Where do you think your fighting and endless conflict come from? Don't you think that they originate in the constant pursuit of gratification that rages inside each of you like an uncontrolled militia? . . . You do not have because you have chosen not to ask." In my case, I didn't have help because I didn't ask for help. Asking for help has always been hard for me. But this time, before I left for Bible study, I took a deep breath and said, "Honey, I'm so thankful for these nights with these incredible women, but it feels really defeating to have a night to myself only to come home and see that all this housework is still waiting for me. It would be really helpful if you could clean up the kitchen after you put the baby down and before you play your games."

You know what he said? "Sure, no problem."

Seriously, it was that easy. As soon as he knew what was bothering me, as soon as I named a way he could help, he was eager to do it. When I came home that night, he was in the kitchen finishing up the dishes. I've hardly seen anything sexier in my life! Then we sat down and I told him about my night. We laughed together, and nobody went to bed grouchy.

When James wrote that we don't have what we want because we choose not to ask, he was referring to praying and asking God for what we want. But does God need us to ask before he can bless us? Of course not. He could certainly give to us precisely what we secretly hope for, because he knows our thoughts. He doesn't need us to ask. Asking, however, changes our posture. Until we ask, until we take the thought out of the mind and bravely name what we really want, we aren't yet in the humble position to receive. Believe it or not, God's primary concern isn't simply to give us what we want. He's after something else—our heart, our character. Asking refines us, makes us aware of our need, and compels us to bow low and wait patiently until we receive. Most often, it's pride that keeps us from asking.

It was certainly pride that kept me from asking Tony to wash the dishes. In my pride, I thought he should think the way that I think and not sit down to relax until all of the chores were taken care of. In my pride, I was unwilling to name how I felt and what I was hoping for; I simply felt entitled to it. But marriage doesn't work that way. In marriage, we have to approach each other humbly. We have to name how we're feeling. We have to ask.

For Discussion:

1   How does each of you feel about asking for help?

2   What makes asking for help easier? What makes it harder?

3   Find out how you could help each other this week.

4   Pray. Ask God to show you where you are being prideful by not asking for help. Ask for humility and wisdom so that you can name what you need and draw closer to each other in the process.

Sweet Kisses

Kiss me with the sweet kisses of your lips,
for your love delights me more than wine.
—Song of Solomon 1:2

Tony was raised a faithful Catholic. I, on the other hand, was raised visiting the First Presbyterian Church just once a year, on Easter, in my pretty new dress and shiny white shoes. When Tony and I were still dating, we'd spend some Sundays in Catholic Mass as I ventured to understand this part of who he was. If you've been to a Mass, you know that the liturgy is well laid out and regular churchgoers know exactly what happens when. I had no Catholic background, so every part of the service was new to me. I relied on Tony to whisper instructions so that I stood at the right times and repeated the right words.

After my first Mass with Tony, I most looked forward to one particular part of the liturgy: the sign of peace. This part of the service is a moment for the congregants to greet each other with a simple message. "Peace be with you," parishioners say to one another. Couples, Tony told me, are allowed—nay, *encouraged*—to kiss one another, in church, in front of everyone. Afterward, he let me know it's mostly for married couples, but though we were only dating at the time, I wasn't going to forget that holy church kiss. I'd gladly be confused and awkward for the entirety of Mass every Sunday, as long as I could still get that tiny kiss in the middle of it.

Keeping communication going in marriage can be a lot of work. Words and intentions can be easily misunderstood. Sometimes we think we've expressed ourselves well but our partner still feels left in the dark. It's easy to feel disconnected and disregarded. Yet there is one simple and wordless way we can communicate love and a desire to be connected to our spouse: a kiss.

We were made to enjoy this trinket of physical intimacy. A kiss, if we kiss long enough, and if we relax into it, opens the eyes of our souls and refreshes the connection we have with our partners. There is power in a kiss, an intimacy reserved for the person you build your life with. Many people have tried to describe the spiritual activity that takes place. Sparks, fireworks, butterflies—whatever metaphors we try to use, the emotion in a kiss is a mystery that has fueled much research.

Based on its research, the Gottman Institute, which studies marriage and relationships, recommends incorporating a six-second kiss into your everyday life. Yep, six whole seconds. Six seconds before or after work. Six seconds in front of the kids. Six seconds before you get out of the car to go into the grocery store together. Six seconds of kissing, if you've been out of the habit, can feel awkwardly long. I usually end up smiling in the middle of it because I kind of want to laugh. Those six seconds remind me that in all of my rushing around, I actually do have time to stop and love my husband and be loved by him. Without those six seconds, I sometimes forget that he is the man I always wanted to kiss.

Remember back to that time in your relationship when all you wanted to do was make out. You settled in to watch a movie together on the couch, but neither of you really cared what movie it was, because you knew you'd spend the whole time kissing anyway. And when your sweetheart wasn't around, you'd spend your time daydreaming about the last time you kissed. As your relationship progressed, it's likely these hour-long kissing fests fell by the wayside. If we're not purposeful, we can lose that simple and powerful way to connect with each other altogether.

My words often fail me. I'm not always great at telling Tony how much I adore him. But sometimes we can say more and connect better in six seconds with a kiss than we can in a drawn-out conversation. Have you had your six-second kiss today?

For Discussion:

1 Go ahead, give it a try. Kiss each other and hold it for six full seconds.
2 Talk about your kiss. Did one of you break first? Did it feel too long? Too short?
3 What other wordless ways do you express your affection?
4 Pray. Thank God he made us *body*, soul, and spirit. Thank him for the power in a kiss and ask him to continue to unify you in all of your physical interactions.

Apologize Like You Mean It

Banish bitterness, rage and anger, shouting and slander, and any and all malicious thoughts—these are poison. Instead, be kind and compassionate. Graciously forgive one another just as God has forgiven you.
—Ephesians 4:31-32

Most mornings, I try to get up early so I can read and think and drink a little coffee before the rest of my family is awake. On one of these mornings, when I got out of the shower and saw my husband, Tony, asleep in bed, my stomach instantly tied itself in knots. The night before, we'd been working together on a project, but we'd had some technical difficulties—our hard drive crashed, there was no ink in the printer, and it was a big irritating mess. As Tony tried to work through the tech stuff, I decided it was all a waste of time and went to bed early.

Now, after a full night's rest, I saw more clearly that I'd been fantastically rude and taken my frustration out on him. I knew I needed to apologize, but I hate apologizing. I mean, why can't I just be grumpy and even a little mean when I feel like it? He shouldn't take it personally, right? I was mad about the computer, not at him! Yet, there he lay, asleep, forgiving me before I even mustered up to the necessary apology. I hated it.

But I slunk back into the bed, nuzzled my face next to his cheek, and I said it: "Will you forgive me for being so rude to you last night? I was a jerk. I'm really sorry."

Wow! That wasn't so bad. As I started saying the words, I began to actually feel them. As I heard myself, I believed what I was saying more and more. I *had* been a jerk, he didn't deserve that, I *was* sorry, and I *did* hope he'd forgive me.

He rolled over toward me and kissed my cheek. "I forgive you," he said. "I love you." And that was it. I was relieved. I couldn't believe how much I'd been dreading apologizing. I had just wanted my bad behavior to go away without me taking any action at all. I'd been so annoyed, but now that it was over, I was light and thankful and even happy. I pranced off to the kitchen to make us some coffee, and the rest of the day was perfectly normal.

Am I the only one who dreads apologizing? Tony's never been that way. He always wants to reconcile as soon as possible. He has no need for grudges, no appetite for bitterness. He wants us to move on and enjoy each other again as fast as possible. His demeanor is always full of grace for me, even when I stumble through an apology.

An apology is usually the turning point in a rift. It's the point at which we switch from heated anger and growing resentment to considering how to grow past an offense. Of course, sometimes my apologies have been weak and have actually made the situation worse. But we can learn to apologize in the way our spouses will best receive it. If you want to say you're sorry in a way that shows you really mean it, here are some dos and don'ts to consider.

The Best Apology

DON'T apologize for someone else's feelings.

"I'm sorry you're mad" is not an apology. It's condescending.

DO apologize for your own actions and attitude.

"I'm sorry I was rude" is an apology that takes ownership. Be specific about what you did wrong. "I'm sorry for whatever made you mad" is *not* going to work.

DON'T add an excuse to your apology.

"I'm sorry I was rude, but I was really irritated" doesn't mean you're sorry. It means you feel justified for the way you acted and you expect to be excused. When you say, "I'm sorry, but . . ." you might just be acting like a sorry butt.

DO ask for forgiveness when you apologize.

"I'm sorry" on its own is just a statement. It requires no response. "Will you forgive me?" is a humble request that can rebuild a relationship. When you ask your spouse to forgive you, wait. Listen. When you're in the wrong, you aren't automatically owed forgiveness. Be grateful when you receive it.

DON'T expect a reciprocal apology.

Do not apologize expecting your spouse to apologize in turn. When you recognize you have done something wrong, just own your part of it.

DO attempt to make a repair.

Once you get through the brutal part ("I'm sorry. Will you forgive me?"), it's wise to take the next step and ask, "Is there anything I can do to make this right?"

For Discussion:

1   Do you dread apologies, or do they usually come easily for you?

2   How did you learn to apologize? What was saying sorry like for you when you were a kid?

3   Ephesians 4:32 says we should forgive one another just as God has forgiven us. When have you needed forgiveness from God? What was it like to receive it?

4   Pray. Ask God to forgive you for anything in the way of your relationship with him and with your spouse. Thank God that he is faithful to forgive us when we approach him, and pray that he increases your capacity to forgive quickly and fully.

Gather

*Let us consider how to inspire each other to
greater love and to righteous deeds, not forgetting
to gather as a community, as some have forgotten,
but encouraging each other.*
—Hebrews 10:24–25

I was still relatively new in my faith when Tony and I started
dating. It was only two years earlier that I'd surrendered to God's
big love and began to pursue him, realizing God had been pursuing me all along. Though he was raised Catholic, Tony had been
out of his Sunday-morning connection to his faith since he was a
teenager. So in the beginning, Tony and I approached spirituality
very differently.

Still, we couldn't deny the connection we had with one
another. I wrestled a lot with whether or not we should even date.
While he was open to attending services with me, it was clear he
was uncomfortable at my church. And even though there was
a little kissing involved at his church (see Week 22), I knew I
wouldn't quite fit in as a Catholic.

Then a friend of mine invited us to come check out their new nondenominational church. Something new to both of us, it turned out, was just what we needed to make that connection with each other. We stayed at that church and eventually both became staff members—Tony worked in music and graphics, while I oversaw groups and membership. And then, after we were married, we moved halfway across the country to help start a new nondenominational church, too. From the beginning, having an open mind toward one another's beliefs and pursuing ways we could explore our faith together were among our top priorities. There's something powerful in connecting with a community of believers. We were thankful to find, and then to help create, a church community where we could both learn and grow.

Granted, Tony and I have gone through periods where we were less faithful in our church attendance, such as after the birth of a child, or during seasons of depression and illness. We know that attending church doesn't make a person any more of a believer than not attending church. However, it's tough to deny that such a habit has a positive impact on couples. According to Harvard researcher Tyler J. VanderWeele, "a number of studies have found similar results: namely, that those who attend religious services are about 30 to 50 percent less likely to divorce than those who do not."

For us, simply attending has not been enough to engage us in community. Wherever we go, we seek out ways to get involved. We commit to serve alongside other people in our church not only to help out, but because we've seen rich relationships grow out of getting to know other people while actively giving our time. Sometimes we serve together, but most of the time we're found on opposite ends of a church building. Tony's skill as a musician usually puts him on stage; my talents keep me looking for ways to be welcoming to others. When we're not volunteering, we get to sit together through a service, worship together, learn together, and be refreshed together.

Participating in community is more than a habit we're committed to. It gives us a chance to practice all of the "one anothers" the Bible calls us to:

> So accept **one another** in the same way the Anointed
> has accepted you so that God will get the praise
> He is due.
> —Romans 15:7

> Don't let selfishness and prideful agendas take over.
> Embrace true humility, and lift your heads to extend
> love to [**one another**].
> —Philippians 2:3

> Make sure no one returns evil for evil, but always
> pursue what is good as it affects **one another** in the
> church but also all people.
> —1 Thessalonians 5:15

No church or community is perfect, mostly because these places are filled with people, like you and me, who bring their baggage, opinions, and ideas. The point isn't to find a flawless faith community, but to find one where you and your spouse can participate, be challenged, and grow together.

For Discussion:

1   What kind of church, if any, did you attend growing up? What was your family's perspective on religious service attendance?

2   How do you each feel about the importance of a faith community now, compared to when you were a child?

3   Besides church attendance, what are some other ways you can participate in your community together and practice the "one anothers"?

4   Pray. Thank God that he designed us to be in relationship with others, not to live this life in isolation. Thank him for your church community if you have one, and ask him to lead you to find one together if you don't. Look for ways to get involved and serve others as a way to invest in your relationship with each other.

Use Your Words

> *Good words satisfy like a fine meal;*
> *yes, good conversations are sure to satisfy.*
> *Words have power in matters of life and death,*
> *and those who love them will savor their fruit.*
> —Proverbs 18:20–21

Mark Twain once said, "I can live on a good compliment two weeks with nothing else to eat." I know the feeling, Mr. Twain— but if I'm honest, I need a lot more than that. If you're the quiet type, it can be easy to dismiss the power of regular verbal encouragement. I remember seeing an old comic strip in which a husband says of marital communication, "I told her I loved her on our wedding day. I'll let her know if anything changes." It's funny, but in reality, that's just not going to work. Compliments, kind words, and little encouragements, shared often, can go a long way to ensure your partner knows they are treasured.

In order to really encourage our partners in a meaningful way, we must pay attention. We need to step outside of ourselves and our perspectives and try to see things the way they do. If we want our words to count, we need to know what's important to the people we're speaking to. This is why specific encouragements are more meaningful than generic ones. "I love the way you did your hair," is far more effective than "You look nice." Both are great, but one shows that you're paying attention.

Tony knows what is important to me. For my very first Mother's Day, he bought me a new car stereo and had it installed. The stereo wasn't on any kind of wish list. It was one of those gifts I wouldn't have thought of for myself, but once I got it, I loved it. But what I loved even more was the lengthy note he wrote me, which took up the left *and* right sides of the Mother's Day card he'd bought. We could have returned the stereo that day, and I would have still been over the moon feeling all the love and appreciation from my husband. His words about what a great wife and mother I was, with details about the things I do for him and our baby that meant so much to him, still bring tears to my eyes. He was thoughtful and specific, and he wrote it all down!

As the book of Proverbs says, good words satisfy. There's nothing better than hearing from the person I love, the person whose opinion matters most to me, that he believes in me and is proud of me. I know my opinion matters to him, too. As partners in life and love, we have immense power to truly encourage each other with our words. We get to speak life to each other and energize each other simply by sharing the specific and wonderful things we notice. We don't need to wait for a special occasion to access this power. All it takes is a tiny bit of good intention and a willingness to notice the good things. Good words are flexible; they can be spoken, whispered, written down, and sent in a text.

If you want to access the positive power of words in your marriage, try some of these ideas:

- Say "I love you," "Please," and "Thank you" every day.
- Be specific in your compliments. Tell your partner you love how gracious he is with your parents, or how she approaches her work with creativity and faithfulness even when it's difficult.
- Say nice things about your spouse to other people. (If word gets back to your spouse, you get double points!)
- Be thoughtful and write something special in the card that goes with a gift. Say you love how nurturing he is with the kids or how resourceful she is in a pinch.
- Think of sticky notes as a pack of hundreds of inexpensive love notes, and use them often.

For Discussion:

1   What is one compliment you've received—not from each other—that has had a lasting impact on you?

2   What kinds of conversations leave you the most energized and refreshed? What are some of your favorite topics?

3   Each of you write five words on five separate sticky notes that describe the characteristics you love most about your partner. Then share them with each other.

4   Pray. Thank God for the partner he's given you. Ask him to help you see each other in new ways, and to help you name the wonderful characteristics that he has cultivated within your spouse.

Be Reconciled

> *It is central to our good news that God was in the Anointed making things right between Himself and the world. This means He does not hold their sins against them. But it also means He charges us to proclaim the message that heals and restores our broken relationships with God and each other.*
> *—2 Corinthians 5:19*

I come from a long proud line of stubborn grudge-holders.

My mother hasn't spoken to her mother in over nine years. I know the exact number because the last time they spoke was when my grandmother came from Texas to Washington for my wedding. My great aunt once let many years pass without speaking to my grandmother or any of my aunts. As far as any of us can tell, she was upset that one of my aunts told her to get out of the way when she was loitering in the kitchen on a bustling Thanksgiving. She stormed out of the house that day, screeching something about being disrespected, and didn't return until my grandfather passed away nearly six years later. They live about four minutes away from each other.

After my own parents' bitter divorce, my mother vowed never to allow my father to see my sister and me for the rest of our lives. The last visit we had with him, I was five years old. Anytime he requested to see us, she refused. Once, when he told her he was coming to town on a particular weekend and demanded he be allowed to see us, my mom took a spontaneous road trip from El Paso, Texas, all the way to Disneyland. I didn't see my father again until I was 22.

Relationships, of course, are complicated, and the underlying current of all of these grudges goes much deeper than I can understand. Every member of my family has their own trebuchet at the ready with a huge pile of ammunition waiting to be hurled at anyone coming their way. It's a never-sorry, easily offended, projectile-firing lineage with an immense capacity to remember who was right and who was wrong—and none of us is ever wrong.

In fact, I was once confronted by a friend about the grudges I was carrying from my childhood. Can you believe that? From two states away, my friend Natalie had the audacity to tell me, "You know, Michelle, if you don't forgive them, the Bible says God can't forgive you." I mean, seriously, the nerve—not only of my friend, but of God! To tell me I needed to work on forgiveness! My hard heart wanted that truth as far away from me as possible. What did Natalie know about what I'd endured? What kind of God would require me to forgive the abuse, neglect, and manipulation I had suffered throughout my life? The one solid lesson I learned from my childhood was to suit up for battle and resist weakness at all costs. What was forgiveness if not weakness? What was apologizing if not conceding defeat in a battle that I had the right to win?

Yet God shows us throughout the Bible that reconciliation is his primary concern. He longs to reconcile humanity into a relationship with himself and wants us to be reconciled with one another. Reconciliation cannot happen without forgiveness, and forgiveness does not happen without practice. What is it to live with a person day in and day out if not the opportunity to practice forgiving each other? Unwillingness to forgive takes a couple from a few minor spats to sleeping in separate bedrooms for years, unable to find their way back to each other. But life doesn't have to be that way.

I no longer see forgiveness as weakness. I no longer see apologizing as conceding. Forgiveness is strength. Forgiveness has the power to restore lives otherwise consumed by bitterness and self-righteousness. I've seen the power of apologies and forgiveness restore my own life. I'm determined now to break that stubborn, grudge-holding lineage. It starts by forgiving the little things, releasing minor offenses, and letting go of the need to be right. Family relationships, friendships, and especially marriages cannot survive if a person who is hurt and offended decides never to lay down the grudges they've been carrying and extend forgiveness.

For Discussion:

1   Were you aware of any feuds or long-standing grudges around your family growing up? What was that like?

2   Is there someone in either of your lives now whom you're holding a grudge against? Talk about that together.

3   What would it take for you to forgive? Is reconciliation something you would consider pursuing?

4   Pray. Thank God for the power of reconciliation demonstrated by his own sacrifice. Ask him to reveal to you any areas of bitterness in your own hearts and to bring healing to those areas, teaching you through the Holy Spirit how to forgive. Pray for the people in your life who have hurt you and ask God to show you how, if at all, reconciliation is possible.

Forgive One Another

> *Therefore, if you are bringing an offering to God and you remember that your brother is angry at you or holds a grudge against you, then leave your gift before the altar, go to your brother, repent and forgive one another, be reconciled, and then return to the altar to offer your gift to God.*
> *—Matthew 5:23–24*

We're bound to inflict pain on one another once in a while. We are flawed and broken human beings, so we end up hurting each other, sometimes carelessly and sometimes purposely. Forgiveness, then, is essential for relationships to continue. Stubborn people like me find it nearly impossible to apologize. Fortunately, my husband is far less stubborn than I am. Sometimes he'll even e-mail me an apology.

Subject: This Morning

I'm sorry.

This morning was my fault. I was sincerely interested in hearing the end of the story, and there was another that came up that I want to hear, but I was late again for my first bus. I was trying to multitask, but I should know better.

That was really hurtful of me, and I can see how asking you a question and walking out of the room was a jerk move. I was planning on listening to you just as I walked quickly to the kitchen and back, but I didn't verbalize that, and therein made you feel ignored and unimportant.

I am so in love with you, and I treated you poorly. I'm so sorry.

Tony

This guy is a pro, right? Like he said in his e-mail, he had asked me a question and then walked out of the room while I attempted to answer him. I was miffed. Then, before I knew it, I heard him locking the door and driving off for work. I couldn't remember the last time he left the house without saying goodbye and giving me a kiss, let alone just walking out after asking me a question and ignoring me.

He called from the road, and I said, "What the heck?" I told him how I felt, and he told me he was sorry, and I said, "Yeah, I gotta go." He's a pro at apologizing; I'm a pro at hearing him apologize and still being angry.

As I wrote in the previous week's devotion, I've got lots of training. It's in my blood as a stubborn grudge-holder. So I stewed—even after I knew that he was sorry—that I would need to forgive him, and that it really wasn't that big a deal. I stewed for another hour or so. Then I sent him a kissy face emoji and he responded with the single dot we send each other as shorthand for "I'm here, and I'm thinking about you." And we both knew we were okay.

To forgive, at its core, is to cancel a debt. The reason we struggle is that when someone offends us, we have this sense that the offender owes us something. Maybe we're owed an apology. Maybe we're owed something more tangible, like a new pair of shoes since he accidentally threw away the pair you just bought, box and all, as he was straightening up the house. (Yes, this really happened.) When we forgive someone, we're telling them and ourselves that they no longer owe us anything at all. The debt is canceled. This doesn't always feel like the right thing to do because, well, if we're owed something, shouldn't we be paid? Wouldn't that be fair?

The trouble is that when we're hurt or offended, it's not likely that any sort of payment or apology will really cover the debt we feel we are owed emotionally. The level of frustration can feel so great that even if we're "compensated," we still have to choose to forgive before we are relieved of it. When we forgive, we take the responsibility away from the offender to fix how we feel.

Deciding to put my faith in Jesus all those years ago meant, first and foremost, that I was a forgiven person. Forgiven for things I knew I needed to be forgiven for and even for things I was unaware of. Forgiven completely: no debt, no interest payments. If you've ever been forgiven for anything big—let off the hook for a car accident that was your fault, not fired even though you were caught stealing money, forgiven by your best friend for sleeping with her boyfriend—then you might have a small sense of the relief I felt. I was keenly aware that Jesus didn't owe me forgiveness, and the truth that I received it anyway was overwhelming. It still is. All of us are more sinful than we imagine, and more loved than we could ever comprehend.

Since God reaches for us first, offers forgiveness first, reconciles us to himself first, he models for us the beauty and strength found in forgiveness. His love shows us that the grace he offers has no limit, and because he doesn't withhold forgiveness from us, we are called not to withhold it from one another.

For Discussion:

1   When was the last time you did something careless that you knew you needed to apologize for? What was that like?

2   Have you ever tried to move past an offense between you and another person without going through the process of apologizing and forgiving? How did that go? Would you say that relationship is thriving or stunted?

3   Pray. Thank God for his boundless forgiveness. Ask him to soften your heart so that you can be better forgivers in your marriage. Thank God for giving you the gift of marriage to let you practice apologizing and forgiving often, staying humble toward one another.

On the Defense

> *The Anointed One suffered for us and left us His*
> *example so that we could follow in His steps. When*
> *He was verbally abused, He didn't return the abuse;*
> *when He suffered, He didn't make threats to cause*
> *suffering in return; instead, He trusted that all would*
> *be put right by the One who is just when He judges.*
> *—1 Peter 2:22–23*

"It's so hard to be around them sometimes. They get so defensive if I say anything at all." I was complaining to Tony, whom I'd just started dating at the time, about a couple of people I was working with.

"Yeah," he said innocently. "You can be pretty defensive, too."

I'm sorry, what? I thought. *Did he just tell me that I'm defensive? I AM NOT DEFENSIVE! Wait ... am I? I'm falling in love with this guy, and I think he feels the same way about me, AND he thinks I'm defensive? Maybe I am. How did I not know this about myself?*

Since then, I've remembered his words and tried to be much more thoughtful about the way I respond to situations and comments that frustrate me. I think he's right; I am naturally defensive. But who isn't? Doesn't everyone want the chance to defend themselves when they feel insulted, misunderstood, or attacked?

Defensiveness is how we react when we feel or fear that we're not fundamentally safe. For most of us, it's automatic, and often rooted in the things that made us feel unsafe, unsupported, or unloved as children. Your level of defensiveness within your marriage often comes from a pattern in the way you and your partner communicate. It is likely that you have built up triggers over time. Maybe the way he sighs automatically causes tension in your neck and shoulders. Maybe the look she gives you as you're disciplining the kids sparks a feeling of frustration. Maybe you're expecting to hear criticism or be attacked for the way you're doing something.

Wherever it comes from, once we realize we're in the habit of being defensive, it's important to realize that this reactionary behavior is not making our relationships stronger. Defensive behavior communicates that you and your partner are at odds instead of on the same team working together. Typically, being defensive is a way to deflect responsibility and instead place blame. But if it's a mostly automatic reaction, what can a person do?

When you recognize you're feeling defensive, stop and say something. I have said, after taking a deep breath, "I think I'm feeling defensive. I think it's because I feel misunderstood and criticized. Can you give me a minute?" Just saying it aloud can have a huge calming effect. Remind yourself that you and your spouse are on the same team and working together is the goal.

When you feel offended, rather than taking your spouse's words as a personal affront, take the opportunity to learn more about how they are feeling. When I approach Tony with my frustrations over all the housework, he could throw up his hands and say, "That's not my fault. I never said you had to do all of those things." Instead, my complaints are usually met with understanding and love. He listens, and that's often enough to start to defuse the situation.

Now, if your partner is the one acting defensively, calling it out is not always helpful. Telling someone, "You're being defensive" will probably make the situation worse. Remember that they're likely behaving this way because they feel attacked somehow and think they need to protect themselves. Rather than attacking further by telling them they're handling the situation poorly, think for a moment about what may have happened to cause this reaction. Again, the goal is to be on the same team, and it takes work to get there.

Instead of accusing your spouse of defensiveness, you could say, "Honey, I love you. I don't mean to sound critical/harsh/insensitive or make you feel attacked. I do want to be able to talk about the issue we're discussing without being completely at odds with each other. How are you feeling right now? What can I do to make this better?"

When you're on the receiving end of an attack, it's not so easy to stay calm. The Bible tells us that, while he was being verbally abused, Jesus did not retaliate. He was able to stay focused because he was confident in who he was and in whom he trusted. The more secure we are in our relationship with God, the less time we'll spend feeling defensive. When we know who we are and in whom we trust, the reactionary need to defend ourselves is replaced by the divine need to have peace and understanding in our relationships. Only then, when we let go of self-righteousness, do we have the perspective we need to be able to turn the other cheek.

Above all, when it comes to defensiveness or any other bad communication habit, it's vital to remember this: People change when they want to, not when we want them to. Creating a supportive, loving, and safe environment within your marriage can go far toward minimizing or even eliminating defensiveness altogether.

For Discussion:

1 Are you aware of triggers, phrases, or actions that make you feel defensive? Are there areas where you feel unsafe, unloved, or unsupported?

2 What can you do together to foster a supportive, grace-filled environment in your marriage?

3 Go back to the Think Like a Team chart at the end of Week 10 (page 62). Which of the phrases from the Individual/Opponent side seem defensive? How can a same-team mind-set help in those situations?

4 Pray. Thank God for being our great defender. Ask him to show you where you may be putting up walls in your lives by being defensive. Ask him to help you let those walls come down and receive each other with more openness and grace.

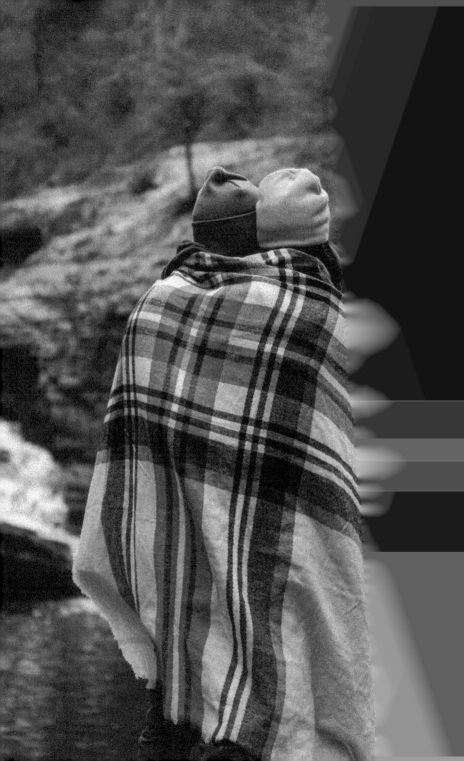

The Empathy Two-Step

Finally, all of you, be like-minded and show sympathy, love, compassion, and humility to and for each other—not paying back evil with evil or insult with insult, but repaying the bad with a blessing.
—1 Peter 3:8–9

Sometimes I feel like my husband and I are having the same arguments on repeat. I hate asking for help, but if I don't ask, he doesn't automatically know what I need. I grumble, he tries to figure out what the problem is, he gets frustrated that I don't come right out and say what's on my mind, and I get frustrated that I have to say anything at all.

"Why don't you see what I see?" I say. "Why do I always have to ask you for help?"

"I see other things," he responds. "The garbage, the lawn, the bills—I don't expect you to see those things. You know if you just say something, I'm happy to help."

"I know! I just hate asking all the time!"

Rinse and repeat.

The good news is there isn't any research that indicates that a healthy marriage is one without conflict. In fact, according to Dr. John Gottman, author of *The Seven Principles for Making Marriage Work*, about 70 percent of arguments in marriage aren't resolvable. As hard as a couple might try, no solution can be found. For many years, psychologists believed that compromise was the answer. But research shows that compromise can create resentment, further driving a wedge between two people. The solution, it turns out, is found in empathy. More important than compromise is that both partners believe they're fully understood. Being heard can relieve the tension even more than working and fighting to reach a mutual agreement.

Empathy is the ability to understand and share the feelings of another person, incorporating precisely the mind-sets that the Apostle Paul exhorts us to work on: love, compassion, and humility. Empathy is a skill that lets us escape our selfish perspectives and imagine what someone else might be experiencing. It requires us to drop feelings of defensiveness so that we can enter into a conversation with grace, repaying even a bad attitude with a blessing of kindness.

Responding to your spouse with empathy, especially if it's not your usual habit, can be a lot like dancing with someone for the first time. Remember in those middle-school PE classes when, for a few weeks, you focused on learning a few dances instead of how to play badminton or run relays? You had to dance with whoever the PE teacher paired you up with, and it was always embarrassing. The first few steps together were the worst:

Do I look in his eyes? Or at my feet, to make sure I'm not about to step on him? Why are we even learning this? None of us are going to dance the Texas two-step at the school dance!

Years later, I see something different, something more than just awkwardness. During those dance lessons, I was learning how to lead and how to follow. I was learning to communicate in the midst of vulnerability without using words. I was learning to stay in that discomfort and keep moving forward instead of running away.

Exercising empathy is a lot like learning those old-fashioned dance steps. It can feel awkward and cumbersome and labored and silly. But over time, if you practice, it begins to feel natural and lovely instead of torturous. You can move through this dance of empathy and enjoy your partner, and you can even stop pretending like you're only doing it because you have to. Practicing empathy is not as complicated as it sounds. It just takes two simple steps.

The Empathy Two-Step

Why does this work? Well, when Tony does this with me, I find I'm much more inclined to honor the fact that he's entering into the situation and trying to figure it out. I also feel invited to express myself to him. And when I try it with him, it works the same way. The point isn't to guess the exact right thing, or even the exact right feeling. The point is to try. Try to engage with your spouse and to attempt to understand how they might be feeling instead of doing what might seem easier, which is to ignore or avoid them. The point is to be like-minded and show sympathy, love, compassion, and humility toward each other.

The Empathy Two Step

When you notice a shift, when your partner seems mad or frustrated, try this...

Why it works: You don't have to guess the correct reason for the emotional change, or even the correct emotion, for this method to work. It works because you are willing to try. You are inviting them to be heard and understood, which is a fundamental craving for all of us.

For Discussion:

1   Describe a time when you felt your partner was really trying to understand where you were coming from. How did that feel?

2   It's tough to show empathy when we're feeling defensive. What simple way can you remind yourselves and each other that you're on the same team?

3   If your partner tried this empathy two-step with you, how do you think you would respond?

4   Pray. Thank God for giving us a spirit of unity. Pray that he would help you be like-minded and humble, ready to defuse frustrations instead of escalating them.

Jumping Lights and Jammies

So imitate me, watch my ways, follow my example,
just as I, too, always seek to imitate the Anointed One.
—*1 Corinthians 11:1*

Our oldest daughter was a January baby, so I had nearly a year to dream up the perfect first Christmas for her. Before she was born, I worked at a hundred-year-old Presbyterian church, rich with traditions I'd never heard of. One of those traditions was Advent, with its special wreath, symbolically colored candles, and themes and verses for each week leading up to Christmas. As a new mom, I wanted to have a picturesque Christmas with my little baby, and developing our own Advent tradition seemed just right.

I researched what Advent really was and how people celebrate it, then got crafty and made my own version of the wreath and a little box that held cards reminding us what verses to read and what to pray for each week. The first year was serene. I held my 11-month-old as she gazed at the lit candle and Tony played a hymn on the acoustic guitar. It was perfect.

The following years brought more babies, and those babies turned into toddlers, and somehow none of them were interested in peacefully watching us light candles or read the Bible or sing hymns. They tried to touch the flames on the candles, talked during the stories and verses, and ran around the house playing while I tried to gather them for singing. It was never again the serene picture of Christmas peace I'd imagined.

Unlike our oldest daughter, our youngest was born on December 1. That season, with three girls under four years old, I was more willing to let go of the perfect Christmas images I'd imagined. One night, after we'd already gotten everyone in their pajamas and ready for bed, Tony and I had a crazy idea. We decided to load up our little sweeties and take them to see some Christmas lights. There was a church nearby with an incredible light display and even a little cottage handing out hot cocoa and candy canes. It was so cold that night, but I can still feel the warmth between my lips and my tiny girl's forehead, the baby carrier keeping us nuzzled together. Tony and I walked behind our little toddlers in their cozy pajamas, coats, and winter hats. We were content to watch them as they marveled at the moving lights and music.

The following year, as soon as the girls started noticing Christmas lights decorating houses, they began asking about their favorite Christmas memory from the year before: "Mama, when are we going to see the jumping lights in our jammies?" So just a few nights before Christmas, we got them in their pajamas, loaded them up in the car, and took them to see the light display.

Getting home that night and watching all three girls giggle and roll around on my bedroom floor, high on late-night sugar cookies and cocoa, I realized that this is how traditions are born.

Throughout the Old Testament, God called his people to set up monuments and to celebrate feasts and festivals as a way to remember their history and their faith. He did not call them to start traditions just for the sake of having something to do annually. No, these traditions were a way to commemorate and celebrate what God had done for the Israelites. Passover serves as a reminder of the day when God intervened, rescuing his people from bondage in Egypt. The tradition is a reminder that binds people together from one generation to the next, passing on the most valued aspects of a unique culture.

Creating your own family traditions is one of the blessings of leaving your parents' house, joining your life with another's, and forging a family of your own. I tried, in vain, to manufacture traditions that would help us bond. We may revisit Advent as the girls get older, but in the meantime, we relish the "jumping lights and jammies" tradition that sprang up naturally. It connects us with stories of the first time we had three little girls to celebrate with and gives us something simple to look forward to each year.

However you come upon them, having traditions of your own is an important part of creating your unique family culture. Remembering where we've been and looking forward to where we'll be next is a powerful way to bond with our partners, create the life we want to live now, and pass our love on to the next generation.

For Discussion:

1   What were some of your favorite traditions growing up? Were there any traditions you dreaded?

2   Do you and your spouse have any traditions that you keep just between the two of you around holidays or anniversaries? Talk about them together.

3   Are there new traditions or rituals that you're interested in exploring together? What would that look like?

4   Pray. Thank God for his provision in your life. Recall a time when he showed up for you, and express your gratitude. Pray that he would continue to unify the two of you through traditions and rituals and that your bond would grow ever stronger.

Handling Small Things

> *For where your treasure is, there your heart will be also.*
> *—Matthew 6:21*

You know that game where you ask someone what they would do if they won the lottery? I'm terrible at that game. I have no imagination for large sums of money. But I do love watching other people win large sums of money in real life, and I think people like me are the reason why Ellen DeGeneres is always giving stuff away on her show.

Once I watched an episode in which an 11-year-old Australian girl named Sabre shared what it was like for her to win $500 in her latest surfing competition. She gave $100 to each of her three siblings, then brought the remainder on her trip to America, where she spent part of it on a Hershey's Kiss "as big as my head" and a pair of socks. She only wished she were richer so she could go to Las Vegas, "because I did research about this place, and there must be a buffet in every single hotel. Like, you can get Krispy Kreme donuts for breakfast! And lava cake for breakfast! And crab legs for breakfast!"

Well, you know Ellen—soon, Sabre is screaming and jumping up and down because Ellen is sending her and her mom to Las Vegas with $500 to spend on buffets (and tickets to see Justin Bieber). The audience was screaming, too, and I'll admit I smiled and shed a few tears watching the whole thing, even though I wasn't the one eating at buffets in Las Vegas or going to see Justin Bieber. Joy and generosity are contagious, aren't they?

When it comes to money, some people find it easy to imagine what they would do if they had more. What would you do with an extra $500 right now? Would you be like Sabre, sharing with your family first and then spending the rest on food? Would you save or invest it? Would you pay down a debt?

In Luke 16:10–11, Jesus says, "If you're faithful in small-scale matters, you'll be faithful with far bigger responsibilities. If you're crooked in small responsibilities, you'll be no different in bigger things. If you can't even handle a small thing like money, who's going to entrust you with spiritual riches that really matter?"

"A small thing like money"? Isn't money a pretty big thing? In many ways, yes, but what Jesus is telling us is that, relative to relationships and spiritual riches, money is small. So why are disagreements over money one of the greatest predictors of divorce? It turns out it's our attitudes about money, not the money itself, that causes these rifts.

Rather than dreaming up what we would do if only we had more, Jesus wants us to first be faithful with what we have now. This is especially important in marriage, where our finances are inextricably linked. If you don't want money to be the thorn in your relationship, look at these four questions and answer them together.

1. **Whose money is it?** The way you answer this question will have a huge impact in how you treat one another when it comes to your finances. Is the money in your family treated as "yours" and "mine," or is it "ours"? What does that look like when it comes to your bank accounts and budgeting?

2. **Where is the money going?** If you don't know where the money is going, it's going to be very hard to have a constructive conversation about it. When was the last time you looked at your bank statement together to evaluate what you're truly spending your money on?

3. **Where do you want your money to go?** As the Cheshire cat once told Alice, if you don't care where you're going, "then it doesn't matter which way you go." When it comes to our finances, we should be telling our money where to go instead of wondering where it went. As a couple, do you know what you want to spend your money on and where you want it to go?

4. **Are your hearts aligned?** If you really want to know what you value, look at what you spend your money on. You could clear up whose money it is, where it's actually going, and where you'd like it to go, but until you determine with your partner that you're on the same page about your financial values and priorities, you're still going to be on shaky ground when it comes to how money impacts your marriage. Take some time to dream together and talk with one another about what is important to you. Do you value

your marriage, your family, and your relationships with others more than you value money? If so, what does that look like practically in your life? How does your spending reflect your values?

For Discussion:

1. Along with discussing the four previous questions, read Matthew 6:19–34. What do you think Jesus is trying to teach us about money in these verses?
2. What financial hurdle(s) did you face as a couple in the early days of your relationship? How did you tackle that hurdle? What could you have done better?
3. How had the things you struggle with financially changed as your relationship has grown and your responsibilities have increased (kids, career, etc.)? How have they stayed the same?
4. Pray. Thank God for the ways he has provided for your family. Ask him to help you have his perspective on money—its usefulness as well as its pitfalls. Pray that you would have peace and unity as you enter this conversation about finances together.

Open Your Ears

> *Listen, open your ears, harness your desire to speak,*
> *and don't get worked up into a rage so easily, my*
> *brothers and sisters.*
> —*James 1:19*

Author and theologian David Augsburger said, "Being heard is so close to being loved that for the average person, they are almost indistinguishable." Great conversationalists know this to be true. All you have to do is ask one or two pretty good questions and then let the person in front of you talk. Look at them, ask them to share more, and they'll walk away believing the two of you have really connected, even if you didn't share much about yourself. People long to be heard. We crave to know that someone out there wants to draw out what's inside of us. I know I do.

I lean toward being an introvert, and part of that, for me, means I don't want to talk unless I'm really sure someone is listening. For the most part, I don't believe people *are* listening, and I've even come up with a little trick to prove it. Sometimes someone will ask me a question and I'll begin to share a story. If I have a sense that they aren't truly listening, I'll stop sharing mid-sentence. I might pause for a second or two, and then ask them a question or change the subject entirely. Most of the time, people won't even notice that I didn't finish what I was saying—they weren't listening. But you know who nearly always notices? My husband. He's listening. When he doesn't catch me, I consider it an indicator that this isn't a good time to talk. He's distracted, so I might revisit the story another time.

I'm not suggesting you try my little trick for yourself; I'll admit it's a little manipulative and passive-aggressive. But it has helped me see that people have short attention spans and listening is hard. The convenience of technology and the advantages of being connected at all times actually seem to be making it harder, not easier, to engage with each other. We're becoming people who are physically present, but mentally elsewhere. We're missing out on listening to and learning from the people in arm's reach.

Listening requires patience and practice, and most of us just aren't skilled at it. But could we be? Could we detach ourselves from our smartphones and laptops long enough to try? If what David Augsburger said is true and being heard is almost equivalent to being loved, shouldn't we practice being better listeners?

Here are some strategies that you can incorporate into your marriage, or any relationship, to become a better listener:

1   **Put down your phone.** Go ahead, put it down. Become aware of how often you instinctively reach for it, and try to stop yourself. Your phone might need a daily curfew while you develop the habit of focusing on each other.

2   **Keep your mouth closed and your eyes open.** When some-
    one does start to talk to you, whenever possible, stop
    talking and look at them. I've been guilty of being an inter-
    rupting listener. I used to think that was how conversations
    went—*we're both talking and listening at the same time;
    I'm relating with you.* But having someone interrupt you,
    even if they think they're only finishing your thought, can
    be frustrating. It's also obvious to people when you're just
    waiting for your turn to talk. With your mouth closed and
    eyes open, try to just listen.

3   **Listen for understanding.** You don't have to agree with
    what you hear, or even believe it, to listen with the goal of
    understanding. If you don't understand what someone is
    saying, ask for clarification. It's a humble thing to do and
    can help them believe they're truly being listened to.

4   **Slow down your response time.** Allow a breath or two
    before you respond to what is being said to you. Give your-
    self time to really take in what the other person is saying,
    and consider if what you're about to say acknowledges
    their thoughts or merely makes your own point. When
    someone is sharing, they aren't always looking for an
    answer or advice from you. Sometimes they're just sharing
    to reveal something of themselves.

We practice the things we want to become better at.
Listening is something most people believe they're already good
at, so it's often not something we think we need to practice. It's
much easier to identify when someone is not listening to us than
to admit we're not really giving our own undivided attention. But
we need to take responsibility for connecting with those we love

through focused listening. Become aware of the things that distract us. Close your game of Candy Crush; leave your phone in another room. You may be surprised at what you learn about the one you love and how much more loved that person will feel.

For Discussion:

1   Who do you know, besides each other, who's a really good listener? Describe this person and how you feel around them.

2   Have you ever realized that you weren't being listened to? What happened? How did you respond?

3   Do you agree with David Augsburger? Does being listened to make you feel loved? What do you think about his observation?

4   Pray. Before you begin, hold hands, take a deep breath together, and allow some silence to enter the room for a few moments. Then, when it seems right to you, thank God that he still speaks to us in these small silent moments. Pray that you would be more sensitive to silence as a way to engage and listen, and ask God to meet you both there. Pray that your capacity to listen patiently would grow, and that by listening you would learn more about each other and love each other better over time.

Come to Me

> *Show me your lovely form. Let me hear your beautiful*
> *voice, for it sounds so sweet, and your face is so lovely.*
> *—Song of Solomon 2:14*

When Tony and I were engaged, I went away on a women's retreat. Being engaged is kind of a funny season; at least it was for me. People who hadn't paid much attention to me before suddenly had all kinds of advice and suggestions about my upcoming marriage. On this women's retreat, I found myself in a room full of mostly married women sharing wedding night stories. I stayed in the corner hoping not to be noticed, even though they all seemed to believe that, as a newly engaged woman, I was the one benefiting from this lively chatter. While the other ladies were swept up in their own funny stories, my friend Jackie, who had been married for a decade at that point, leaned over to me and quietly said something I'll never forget: "Don't worry too much about your wedding night. It might be amazing, but it might not. I just want you to know, whatever happens, sex gets so much better over time."

What Jackie said was unlike any other opinion or advice I was hearing at the time. She tapped into a truth about intimacy that I had yet to discover for myself. When you hear the word *intimacy*, your mind might go straight to "sexy time." Intimacy is that, but it's also much more, because sex is much more than what happens between two naked bodies. Intimacy is what occurs when two people who have chosen to be naked in front of each other bare their souls and share the wonderful and scary things that make them feel vulnerable.

Intimacy begins in the mind and is cultivated in loving, open conversation. Then, when your bodies meet, there is nothing left but to enjoy the gift of sex that God has created for us. It's a gift that waits to be opened when we have spent our energy creating a safety-net atmosphere in our marriage, an atmosphere where mistakes are made and recovered from with grace, an atmosphere in which we know we are accepted and loved even when we're at our worst. This is the kind of atmosphere that takes years to nurture and cultivate. It's that knowing, loving, and history of being real and raw and vulnerable with each other in daily life that makes sex better and better as the years go by. We must be able to be open with each other about our triumphs, about our failures, and about sex itself.

Song of Solomon is a beautiful anthem in the Bible that shows us a picture of a couple who moves from courtship to consummation. In it, we find a man and a woman professing their desire for one another. He says to her, "Now, my dove, don't be shy. Don't hide from me in the clefts of the rock or nest like a bird in secret among the cliffs. Show me your lovely form. Let me hear your beautiful voice, for it sounds so sweet, and your face is so lovely" (Song of Solomon 2:14).

She responds, "My love is mine, and I am his. He grazes among my lilies. As the day breathes its morning breeze and shadows turn and flee, turn to me, my love, like a gazelle; come to me like a young stag on rugged mountains" (2:16–17).

These two clearly adore each other, long for each other, and find no taboo in expressing it. If you and your partner aren't talking about sex, then you're not having the best sex. A team of researchers led by psychologist David Frederick found that one of the key components of sexual satisfaction in long-term relationships is communication about sex. I'd wager it's not necessarily what the couples talk about that increases their satisfaction, but the fact that they're willing to be open and honest about such a vulnerable topic.

Intimacy requires us to be transparent. When you make yourself available to see your partner and truly be seen by them, then you can receive the full spectrum of pleasure and connection. Good, godly sex requires us to be vulnerable with each other, to know we're safe, and thus to fully engage and receive from one another the very best of this beautiful gift.

For Discussion:

1   Read chapter 2 of Song of Solomon aloud together. Talk together about what you think this couple is trying to convey to each other.

2   Ask your partner, "What do you like about our sex life?"

3   Ask your partner, "Is there anything about our sex life you would like to change?"

4   Pray. Thank God that he has made us body, soul, and spirit, and that none of these elements exists without the others. Pray that as you engage with each other, exploring intimacy in all its facets, your spirits and souls would connect as your bodies touch. Thank him for the blessings of pleasure and connection.

Can I Trust You?

*Most people claim to be loyal, but can anyone
find a trustworthy person?
The right-living act with integrity.*
—Proverbs 20:6–7

Trust is foundational for all relationships, but especially for marriages. Sometimes, though, trust is not so easy to cultivate, and
once broken, it can be excruciatingly difficult to repair.

Some people come by trust naturally. I have a friend, Emily,
who sincerely believes the best of people and is absolutely
crushed when someone doesn't live up to that belief. Her attitude
makes sense to me because I know her parents; they've been
married for a million years, they've stuck together for better or
worse, and they love and support Emily and her three sisters like
crazy. Of course Emily would be trusting and joyful.

For others, like me, trusting people can feel foolish and
uncomfortable. We've been let down profoundly in the past, and
we have a hard time believing that people have good intentions

and will follow through. This general belief that nobody is truly trustworthy can cast a shadow over all of our interactions.

But trust can be learned over time and carefully cultivated within a relationship. The first step is to become a trustworthy person; it's difficult to trust others if you don't trust yourself. People who instill trust in others share these five characteristics:

The Five Characteristics of Trust

1 **Integrity.** Integrity means doing the right thing at all times and in all circumstances, whether or not anyone is watching. It means having the same values at work as you do at home and around your friends. Do you hold the same values no matter where you go? Will you act on what you believe?

2 **Honesty.** When you hold the same values in all circumstances, it's easy to tell the truth. Do you say what you mean or omit important details? Of course, everyone is prone to slip and tell a lie or exaggerate once in a while, but an honest person will own up to the lie and admit the truth. Are you honest about who you are and what you believe, or do you change your answers based on who's listening and what's convenient?

3 **Consistency.** Like integrity and honesty, consistency is a crucial factor in building trust with others. Are you considered reliable, or would people say you're pretty flaky? In his book *The Speed of Trust*, Stephen M. R. Covey writes, "One of the fastest ways to restore trust is to make and

keep commitments—even very small commitments—to ourselves and to others." This is the kind of consistency that builds trust others can rely on.

4   **Intent.** Covey includes a Gandhi quote in *The Speed of Trust*: "The moment there is suspicion about a person's motives, everything he does becomes tainted." People need to believe that your intentions are good and that you will act on them no matter what. Mistakes may happen and things may go wrong, but if those around you can point to a track record of your sincerely good intentions and actions, you will easily be forgiven.

5   **Transparency.** How would you feel if anybody and everybody listened in on your conversations? How would you feel if your spouse were browsing your text messages and e-mails? I'm not endorsing snooping, but if you're trustworthy, almost nothing in your communications to anyone should need to be so private that you couldn't share it openly and willingly with your partner. Of course, there are gifts and surprises that we would like to keep private for a time, but aside from those circumstances, full disclosure is critical in building trust with people who are important to you.

So how do you fare? Would you give yourself a gold star, or are there areas you could improve? It's easy to point the finger at other people, even your partner, but becoming trustworthy is the first step in building trust in your relationship.

If, however, you feel jealousy and distrust even though your partner shows a lot of trustworthy characteristics, you have a different route to take. In order to build trust, you need to practice trusting. You cannot grow past your natural distrust until you give your partner room to show you that they are, in fact, trustworthy.

We all want to be trusted. We all want to be with people who are trustworthy. It's important because once we're trusted, once we're believed in, we are given more freedom and grace than we ever thought possible. When you're trustworthy, nobody looks at you sideways. Nobody wonders if you mean what you say or if you'll come through on your promise. People speak well of you when you've earned their trust. They'll stand up for you if anyone says anything negative; they'll put themselves on the line.

When we've earned trust, when we've extended trust to others, we fortify our relationships so that they stand firm against any obstacle that might come against them.

For Discussion:

1   Are you more trusting and optimistic, or more untrusting and pessimistic?

2   Which of the five characteristics of trust is most important to you? Explain why.

3   When issues of trust come up, are you more likely to respond openly or defensively? Why do you think you respond this way?

4   Pray. Thank God that he is trustworthy. He is faithful and never breaks his promises. Pray that, through the Holy Spirit, he would cultivate that same faithfulness and consistency in your marriage.

House Rules

Let Me say it again: if you ask for anything in My name, I will do it. If you love Me, obey the commandments I have given you. I will ask the Father to send you another Helper, the Spirit of truth, who will remain constantly with you.
—John 14:14–16

Some say rules are meant to be broken. Tony and I are not those people. We're the kind of people who value clarity and feel we can act more freely within well-defined boundaries. Tony is even more of a rule follower than I am, but we both agree that having certain standards usually benefits our family. The way we see it, there are the people we were when we first met, the people we were when we first got married, the people we are today, and the people we both want to become. Having a sense of purpose and deciding together on some ground rules and family mottos will help us get there together.

We want to be people who are allowed to make mistakes, but also learn from those mistakes. We pass this down to our girls by using the same routine whenever they get in trouble. We put them in time-out, and when it's over, we kneel, they stand, and we ask them to tell us why they were there. It's not a trick question; if they can't tell us, we'll just tell them ourselves. Then we ask them to tell us if what they did was a good idea or a bad idea, and what would be a better idea in the future. Then we pray almost the same prayer every time: "Dear Jesus, please forgive me for calling my sister names [or whatever the bad idea was]. Help me remember to be kind and gentle [or whatever would have been a better idea]. And help Mommy and Daddy be a good mommy and daddy. Amen."

Then we give big hugs and I love yous, and everyone gets to move on. As the girls have gotten a little older, they've started to pray their own words, but their prayers are still pretty similar to what we taught them. That last line is important to us. We want the girls to know that Mommy and Daddy need help to do the right thing just as much as they do. We need to be reminded because we aren't perfect. We ask them for forgiveness when we've been overly harsh or snippy so they see that it goes both ways. We value second chances. Making this a concrete rule helps hold us all accountable, parents and children alike.

We also value generosity. One of our most recited family mottos goes like this: "We share because everything is a gift." When the girls start saying, "That's mine!" it's an easy guideline to recall. All we have to do now is ask, "Claire, why do we share?" and she'll respond, "We share because everything is a gift." We hope it helps her remember, as it helps us, that owning anything is a privilege and everything we have has been given to us as a gift in one way or another. We want to be generous people who raise generous kids. We want to hold onto material things loosely and be ready at all times to give away what we have.

We set these standards not for the sake of following rules but to create a home and a family in which we're all encouraged to become the people we want to be, refined by love, overflowing with grace. That includes Tony and me, which I was reminded of not long ago when I came to him to work through some hurt feelings I was having about a friend. He listened and offered his perspective. Then he said, "Well, we don't retaliate. We don't hold grudges. We don't keep a laundry list of the ways we are hurt or irritated. We forgive, right?" It was an example of the beautiful way he reminds me who I want to be, regardless of how I feel.

These rules are really expressions of characteristics we want for our family. Keeping them in mind helps direct our behavior toward one another as well as the decisions we make together. Other common mottos you might hear around our house include "Serve others first," "Speak kindly," and "Help clean up."

One of the great benefits of being married is being able to start fresh with a family of your own. Maybe you grew up in an idyllic situation and now you're modeling your family after what you experienced. Maybe you grew up in an environment that was harsh, critical, or cold. Now is your chance to do something new. You and your spouse get to decide together what is important and meaningful to you. Tony and I want to be a family of character, a family who is generous and kind, and a family who admits mistakes and asks for forgiveness. What do you want your family to be about? Do the rules and common sayings in your home reflect the people you want to become? You get to decide. Your family, your rules!

For Discussion:

1   What were some common sayings and rules in your home growing up?

2   Are there rules and mottos that you hope to incorporate into your family now? Are there any you want to avoid?

3   Read John 14 in your Bible. What do you think is the relationship between loving God and obeying his commands? In what way can we expect the Holy Spirit to help us?

4   Pray. Thank God that we have an example of loving obedience in his son Jesus Christ. Ask God what kind of person he is refining you to become and if there are rules, mottos, and commands that will serve as reminders to both of you. Pray for the Holy Spirit to guide you in keeping these commandments.

But First, Coffee

> *When a man first gets married, he's free from military service and any other civic duty for one year. He and his wife may spend that year happily together in their home.*
> *—Deuteronomy 24:5*

Now that the girls are getting a little older, mornings no longer begin with crying babies who need diaper changes. The girls are all old enough to get themselves out of bed and ask for what they want. Soon they'll be old enough to start breakfast on their own, too, but not quite yet. When I come into the kitchen in the morning, I'm greeted by three snuggly girls in their pajamas gleefully explaining to me what they want and definitely don't want for breakfast.

"Momma, can I have oatmeal?"

"Momma, I don't want oatmeal. Can I have yogurt?"

"Momma, I don't want oatmeal or yogurt. Can I have cereal with bananas and raisins?"

Do you know what I make first, no matter what? Coffee. They keep asking for things and changing their minds and chattering in the background of my thoughts as I focus on grinding the beans and pouring the water into our faithful coffeepot. Coffee is the priority. I don't apologize for making them wait. Waiting is good for kids. Coffee is good for me. Everything will go much better for everyone if I get this one priority taken care of first thing.

The real trick is to be in the same room with these cuties and not let their requests, demands, and enthusiasm for their first meal derail me from first making the coffee. In the same way, many people make requests and demands of us throughout our days. If we don't have perspective on what our priorities are, it can be really difficult to focus and make sure the most important things in our lives are taken care of first. This is where boundaries come in.

When it comes to your marriage, boundaries are not meant to be walls that shut people out. They're meant to help you properly prioritize your relationships. On Earth, there will never be a relationship more important than your marriage. When you make other relationships—with your parents, children, and sibling or even a job—a higher priority, the marriage suffers. Conversely, when a healthy marriage is your top priority, all of those other relationships can flourish because of it. When your marriage is healthy, you encourage each other to nurture your relationships with your parents and in-laws. When your marriage is healthy, your children have a greater sense of love and security. When your marriage is healthy, your relationships with your siblings and friends benefit from your joy and peace. When your marriage is healthy, you are encouraged to pursue greatness in your work. Once you choose a person to spend your life with, the way you handle that one relationship plays a factor in all the other relationships you encounter. Mixing up your priorities will only push all of the other relationships in your life into chaos.

In Moses's time, men were expected to serve their city and their military while their wives stayed behind to manage the home. But tucked into the book of Deuteronomy among a set of commands about divorce and moneylending is the verse from the beginning of this chapter, which frees men from all civic duties to spend time with their wives for the first year of marriage. Isn't it interesting to require men to set aside their usual priorities in favor of simply being with their wives? I wonder how many of our marriages would be on firmer ground if we all spent that many hours in the very first year of marriage working out the kinks, learning to communicate with each other, and prioritizing togetherness.

Many of us take a week or less after the wedding to be together. We call it a honeymoon. When the honeymoon ends, we're all supposed to get back to "real life." But if real life after the honeymoon doesn't involve shifting priorities so that our marriage comes before all other relationships and responsibilities, we lose focus and can be easily distracted by what everyone and everything else seems to need from us—just like my girls can distract me from making coffee in the morning. In order to thrive in other areas of life, we need to be able to hear the demands and requests of the world around us and tune them out just enough to say to ourselves, "But first, my marriage."

For Discussion:

1   Now that you're married, how have your priorities shifted since your single days?

2   Which relationships or responsibilities in your life make it difficult to prioritize your marriage?

3   Ask each other, "What practical thing can I do to show you that my relationship with you is my first priority?"

4   Pray. Thank God for giving your partner to you and you to your partner. Ask him for wisdom and clarity so that you can navigate all other relationships and responsibilities according to their proper priority in your life. Ask for the strength to gently say no to anything that would try to bump your marriage out of first place.

Bowling with Bumpers

> *Enjoy life with the woman you love. Cherish every moment of the fleeting life which God has given you under the sun. For this is your lot in life, your great reward for all of your hard work under the sun.*
> *—Ecclesiastes 9:9*

In high school, I took a PE class called Individual Sports where we learned games like golf, pool, and bowling. The first time our class showed up at the bowling alley, we noticed that half the lanes had bumpers up and half didn't. If we wanted to keep our ball from going into the gutter, our coach let us use a bumper lane, and about a third of the class did, including me. We may have looked silly, but our scores were way higher than the students who were bowling without bumpers, because, no matter what, we could at least hit one pin with every shot. The others had to try much harder just to keep the ball in the lane, let alone score any points.

The early part of my marriage to Tony was like bowling with bumpers. We set up boundaries, guidelines gleaned from older, wiser couples, to help us stay the course. Those boundaries included avoiding time alone with someone of the opposite sex—no hanging out alone, riding in a car alone, or having friendships our spouse was not included in. Most of the time, these rules were pretty easy to keep up with. Neither of us was trying to make the other feel restricted. We considered the boundaries to be preventive; they were a way to build trust with each other and to protect our relationship from anyone who might want to come between us.

We'd been married less than two years when we moved to Wisconsin. We didn't know very many people and were focused on working hard to help launch a new church. Part of Tony's responsibilities with the church included training and practicing with other musicians. A couple of times when I came home from work I would find Tony practicing music with a woman I'll call "Melissa" in our living room. I was getting to know this young woman just like Tony was, and we both adored her. But something about walking into my own home to find my husband had been spending time alone with another woman made me uncomfortable. It was the first time that the boundaries we set up early on were being tested, and I had to decide how I was going to handle it.

After some prayer and deep breathing, I brought it up to Tony. I felt so nervous; I didn't want to come across as jealous or possessive. Over dinner that night, I started by saying, "Hey, remember when we first got married and we agreed we wouldn't be spending time alone with anyone of the opposite sex? I know that's tricky out here because you don't exactly have a practice space for the music team, but I felt really uncomfortable these last two times that I've come home to find you practicing alone with Melissa. It's not that I don't trust you or her. I just felt uncomfortable, and I'd like to revisit why we set up those boundaries in the first place."

It's been years, but thinking back to that conversation reminds me how uncomfortable I was. Still, we walked into that discomfort together and talked about the challenges he was facing trying to practice music with a team of volunteers who all had differing schedules. I tried to remain understanding and willing to move the boundaries we set up. In the end, we decided that he would continue to invite people into our home to practice, but if there were going to be women there, he would arrange the practice around a time when I would be home. It made things a little complicated for a while, and I had to sacrifice the stillness of my once-quiet home, but we made it work.

The boundaries we set up in the beginning didn't make either of us more trustworthy, just like bumpers in bowling didn't make me a better bowler. What they did instead was give us an opportunity to practice prioritizing our marriage above all other relationships. They helped us be clear about what was acceptable and what wasn't. Our boundaries helped me bring up a topic I was uncomfortable with, because my concern was based on something we both agreed on initially.

Now, 10 years into our marriage, I feel less concerned about the boundaries we set up initially. We have spent years building trust in our marriage and holding to the kind of boundaries that help us demonstrate that there is nobody more important to us than each other. Building this love together requires us both to work and sacrifice, but it also enables us both to enjoy the fruit of our labor: a marriage that is safe and fulfilling.

For Discussion:

1   Were there rules and boundaries you had to follow as a kid that you didn't appreciate then but do appreciate now? What were they? How has your perspective changed?

2   Read Proverbs 5 in your Bible together. In verse 18, the reader is encouraged to "know true joy with the wife of your youth." What sort of boundaries could help create that true joy?

3   Have you ever decided together on boundaries that would build trust in your marriage? If so, revisit them. How do you feel about them now? If not, think together about the sorts of boundaries you can agree on that would build trust for you.

4   Pray. Thank God for the guidance you've received that has acted as a guardrail to keep you on a path of fruitfulness and joy in your life. Ask God to reveal to you the areas of your life that still need boundaries so that you can keep your marriage as your first priority. Thank him for the trust that already exists between you and your spouse, and pray that it will increase in the years to come.

Foreign Ambassadors

My friend, you demonstrate your faithfulness in all the things you do for the brothers and sisters; even when they are strangers to you, you treat them as family.
—3 John 1:5

I was maybe four years old the first time I went to Mexico. Driving into Juárez, the city where my mom and aunts had spent much of their childhood, I expected it to look just like our little neighborhood in east El Paso. Everyone in my family spoke Spanish at home, and I knew most everyone in Juárez would be speaking Spanish, too. Still, as a child, I relied on my grandmother to help me navigate this new place with these new people.

Though I'd been eating Mexican food and listening to conversations in Spanish for as long as I could remember, I recognized instantly that Juárez was not like home. The smells were different, the way people drove was different, and the street tacos were better than any tacos I'd tasted in Texas.

At that age, I was lucky to be learning some Spanish at home, but I was thankful to be able to tug on my grandmother's hand nervously whenever someone new spoke to me. She leaned down and whispered a translation: "She wants to know if you'd like a cookie, Micha. Would you?" "Gracias," I said, smiling and nodding as I accepted the treat from my grandmother's friend.

Entering into the world of in-laws is a lot like entering a foreign country for the first time. Each family has its own culture rich with its own language, food, stories, and jokes. In the same way that I relied on my grandmother to be an ambassador for me when we visited Mexico, we need to be ambassadors between the person we married and the family we were raised with. It's easy for us to take for granted our unique family culture and think our methods are the norm. But if you've ever been an outsider in a situation, you know the things other people take for granted can take some getting used to for somebody new.

When you get married, you're not only entering a new family culture and bringing your partner into yours, you're forming a new culture together as well. The new family you're creating will be a unique combination of all of the values and traditions you were each raised with, plus whatever new ones you might choose. It's important to remember that your allegiance has shifted. You must prioritize your new family over the family you were raised with, and you must take on the role of ambassador between your family of origin and the family you have now chosen to be a part of. This means that if there's any potential for misunderstanding between your partner and your parents,

it's on you as the ambassador to navigate these tricky waters.
Remember, you're the reason these two cultures have collided
and now need to interact.

The first year I brought Tony to my mom's for Christmas
was the first time I found myself in this role. Just as we walked
in, before we could even get our coats off, my mom was already
explaining to Tony that her computer was broken and she
couldn't figure out what was wrong and could he please take a
look? Ever the kind tech-worker gentleman, Tony made his way
to her office to see what he could do. When I went to check on
him a little while later, I realized my mom's computer problems
were complicated enough to take hours.

This was my opportunity to be an ambassador. I spoke up
to my mom on my new husband's behalf and let her know that,
as much as he'd like to help, she was going to need to take her
computer in to be serviced. Otherwise, Tony was going to miss
Christmas dinner and present opening. My mom was gracious
and thanked him. He was gracious and made some recommen-
dations. Even though it was a small instance, it set the tone for
future interactions between all of us. Tony gets to be the nice
helpful guy, and if there's something disappointing to say, I'll
say it. He does the same thing for me with his family. I get to be
accommodating and helpful, but if something isn't going to work
for us or our kids, Tony is the one who has that conversation with
his family. As ambassadors, we're also there to teach each other
about our family's traditions and customs and explain to each
other some of the history behind strange interactions.

Over time, interacting with your in-laws will feel less like
exploring a foreign land. You'll start to understand your role and

how to be respectful and gracious about a culture that still may feel strange to you. As long as your relationship with your partner is the priority, as long as your marriage is the culture you're most loyal to, the two of you will be able to navigate these foreign delegations as a team with confidence and grace.

For Discussion:

1   Have you ever visited another country, or even another part of your own country? What were some of the major cultural differences you needed help navigating?

2   What were some of the new-to-you differences you noticed about each other's families during your first interactions with them? How did it feel to be the stranger in these situations?

3   What is one of your biggest challenges when it comes to your families and in-laws? How can you help each other navigate these challenges?

4   Pray. Thank God for welcoming us into his family as strangers and making us his sons and daughters. Pray that he would embolden you with grace for each other's families, releasing judgment over differences and equipping you with understanding so that you can be good ambassadors for one another.

Baggage Handling

> *So since we stand surrounded by all those who have gone before, an enormous cloud of witnesses, let us drop every extra weight, every sin that clings to us and slackens our pace, and let us run with endurance the long race set before us.*
> *—Hebrews 12:1*

As a bride, I walked down the aisle alone to meet my groom. It was symbolic: I did not have a father to give me away. I came alone to give myself away. In retrospect, maybe I should have been lugging a huge suitcase down the aisle. Since I was being symbolic, I could have given Tony a better picture of the baggage he was about to commit himself to.

Baggage is anything that you bring into the relationship that has nothing to do with your partner but can cause tension, damage, and strife between the two of you. Addictions, ex-lovers, past abuse, psychological disorders, debt, insecurities—any number of things. Often, they're issues that have gone unresolved, but even personal history that seems under control can show up unexpectedly in the heat of a discussion or argument.

Granted, my husband-to-be could have been waiting at the end of the altar with his own suitcase, and I would have imagined he had only adventurous dreams tucked away inside of it. I wanted to be married to him, and everything in me hoped I could handle my own baggage or keep some of it hidden from him. I knew it was there, and I had shared some of the stories with him, but I didn't want to bring it into our marriage. Except I brought it anyway.

Our little daughters, while they are blessings in every way, have, since their arrival, revealed a new layer of baggage. I'm terrified something horrible will happen to them. It's my worst nightmare that they would experience anything even close to what I went through in my childhood. I was so stressed about it that I actually cried in the locker room the first several times I dropped them off at my gym's childcare. This is the sort of thing I know deserves to be unpacked and confronted, but truthfully, I didn't want to.

Still, for the health of my family and my marriage, I had to recognize how important it is to work through the baggage. Hiding it or pretending it isn't there is not only dishonest, it's also burdensome. When we carry around unresolved issues, they have a way of seeping out into our everyday interactions with our family, and our loved ones ultimately bear more of the burden than we realize. Here are some things I've learned about how to address your baggage:

How to Unpack Your Baggage

1   **Name it.** Whether it's child abuse, overbearing or neglectful parents, addiction, debt, or dashed dreams, it's important to name the things dragging you down. Acknowledge that this is a part of your life that causes you pain. Our baggage, after all, is part of our story as a whole. Even when it's painful, it shapes who we become. Over the years, I've often tried hard to hide my baggage, claiming, "I'm just a private person." The reality is that I have felt ashamed about what happened to me and even more ashamed of the decisions I made on my own as I grew up. However, I've found that as I share with people who are safe (trusted friends, counselors, my husband), the power of shame dissipates, and the blame I lay on myself rises off of my shoulders. Have you named your baggage?

2   **Take responsibility.** Whatever your baggage, it's important to take responsibility for your current behavior. In my case, it was important for me to address the bitterness and inability to forgive I'd been carrying around for years. Tucked into the baggage I carry are the years of sexual abuse from a man in my family whom I looked up to greatly. The man who abused me eventually did acknowledge it, but he has never apologized. Regardless, I've forgiven him and have to practice forgiving him when I feel fear or bitterness rising up in me again. Not because what happened to me was my fault—it wasn't—but because we have to take responsibility for our current behavior, and I can't move forward if I'm living in fear and bitterness instead of godliness. What part of your baggage can you own?

3   **Ask for patience.** When you're married, it's important to bring your spouse into this process. Ask for patience from them as you push through the hard work of confronting your baggage. Be patient with them as they may have a hard time understanding what you're going through. It's important to remember that your spouse is not the initial cause of your baggage, so that you don't project your insecurity, trust issues, or frustrations onto them. Have you asked for patience?

4   **Seek healing.** Whether it's individual counseling or just a good solid mentor, get the help you need. Unpacking your baggage can be a slow and painful process, and I'm continuing to learn how important it is not to attempt to do it alone in the dark. Have you begun to seek healing?

Everyone has baggage of some sort. It's impossible to find someone without any past issues. But it's vital that we release this extra weight so we can move forward in all that God has in store for us. In a loving relationship, we have the opportunity to help each other unpack safely so that we can step forward a little lighter every day.

For Discussion:

1   Your marriage should be the safety net where you can name your baggage without judgment. Have you named your baggage to each other? Do that now.

2   Dysfunctional and unhealthy communication is often the result of unresolved baggage. Can you attribute any of your

bad habits (quick temper, jealousy, aloofness, etc.) to some of the baggage you've been carrying?

3   God promises that he will heal the brokenhearted. Have either of you considered counseling as a means of receiving the healing that you need? What next steps toward healing could you begin together today?

4   Pray. Thank God for accepting us with our baggage and for healing and restoring us. Pray that he would give you grace and patience with each other as you name your baggage, begin to take responsibility for your current behavior, and seek his full and complete healing from all that you carry.

The Fullness of Life

> *I came to give life with joy and abundance.*
> *—John 10:10*

As Tony was getting the girls ready for a bath one night, he called me into the bathroom. Our five-year-old, Claire, had a deep, dark red scratch all the way down her left arm. She looked embarrassed while we inspected her arm to figure out what happened. "I don't want to tell you," she said. "I tried to put some lotion on it...."

We finally figured out she'd been holding our cat, Banda. Banda, you should know, got grumpier each time we added a new member to our little family. We let the kids pet him but warned them that if they weren't gentle, he might react by scratching and biting. Now we were looking at Claire's arm, evidence that she'd not only disobeyed us by holding the cat but also gotten hurt and tried to cover it up.

This is exactly what shame does. Our natural response to shame is to try to hide it, cover it up, and fix it ourselves. If Claire had come to us right away, we could have cleaned the scratch immediately and put some ointment on it. Instead, she tried to hide it, and not knowing any better, put lotion on it in an attempt to take care of it herself. She was afraid she'd be punished, but as her parents who love her, we just wanted to make sure she was okay. We'd warned her about the cat not because we didn't want her to enjoy the cat, but because we knew he could be dangerous. We had no interest in scolding her—that huge red scratch seemed like punishment enough—we just wanted to help her heal. She wasn't going to be able to handle that deep cut on her own. As her parents, it's our job to take care of her, and it's all we want to do.

Likewise, the messages of shame we're each carrying about sex can make sex and intimacy difficult topics to broach. People have been taught, especially in more conservative environments, that virginity is the highest honor, that complete abstinence and even denial of our natural feelings of desire and passion are the only way to live a godly life.

But Jesus, speaking about the difference between what the Devil offers and what he offers said, "The thief's purpose is to steal, kill and destroy. My purpose is to give life in all its fullness" (John 10:10 TLB). Jesus wants us to experience the fullness of love and life. Despite what man-made religion would have us believe, God is not keeping us from experiencing the full benefits of sex. It's shame that takes the joy out of sex. Secrets and shame are the enemies of intimacy. But once shame is spoken, once it is brought into the light and exposed, it dies and makes way for connection and pleasure.

If you're human, you most likely have some baggage around your ideas about sex. Men, for instance, are taught from a young age that it's up to them to initiate sex, which makes them more likely to be on the receiving end of rejection. Most husbands, even if they know their wife's "not tonight, honey" isn't personal, have a hard time not taking it personally once in a while. Women also experience shame and fear of rejection concerning sex. We're comparing ourselves constantly with images of perfect bodies and being told repeatedly that "men are visual." I know many women, myself included, who sometimes say "not tonight, honey" more out of embarrassment about their bodies than a lack of desire for their husbands. Women also sometimes believe the lie that men are so interested in sex that it doesn't matter where they get it. They then see sex as obligatory, less about connection and more about satisfying a biological need. Because intimacy begins in the mind, it's difficult to push past all this rejection and shame in order to allow ourselves to truly engage and connect.

Another myth is that sex before marriage—whether it was consensual or abusive—prevents us from having good, healthy, godly sex within marriage. Do not believe this lie. You were made to love and be loved. Whether or not you were a virgin (however you define that) before marriage does not preclude you from enjoying the full benefits of intimacy.

Shame makes us hide. Keeping secrets creates a wedge in our relationships with each other and with God. Whether we're ashamed of something we've done or of something that was done to us, hiding and covering it up prevents us from healing and experiencing intimacy in our most important relationships. God, being a much more loving parent than Tony and I could ever be to Claire, just wants us all to be whole and healed.

Psalm 103:12 says, "You see, God takes all our crimes—our seemingly inexhaustible sins—and removes them. As far as east is from west, He removes them from us." God's greatest desire for us in marriage is that we would experience the fullness of his love. I believe marriage is meant to be a sanctuary, a place where we encounter Jesus, where we practice forgiveness and being forgiven, where we understand the blessing of being vulnerable with someone who will be careful with us at home, so that we can go out into the world with confidence, knowing we are fully loved.

For Discussion:

1 When did you first have the "sex talk" with your parents? What was that like?

2 Can you identify with any of the shame triggers mentioned—fear of rejection, lack of connection, comparison? Where do you think this comes from?

3 Prolonged skin-to-skin contact releases oxytocin, a feel-good bonding hormone, into the brain and bloodstream. How would you feel about incorporating more skin-to-skin contact with your spouse in your everyday lives?

4 Pray. Thank God for his promise to remove our sin as far away from us as east is from west. Pray that he would unify you as you do the work to dig shame out of your relationship so that you can experience the full pleasure and connection found in marital sex.

Week 41

Contempt Is a Sneaky Devil

Explore me, O God, and know the real me . . .
Put me to the test and watch how I handle the strain.
Examine me to see if there is an evil bone in me,
and guide me down Your path forever.
—Psalm 139: 23–24

The summer sky was endlessly dark above us; stars and land-
marks were absent. Tony and I had only the blue glow of the car
stereo to help us see each other's faces on the long drive from
Washington state to our new home in Wisconsin to start a new
adventure. We were somewhere in the middle of Wyoming
listening to an audiobook: *Blink*, by Malcolm Gladwell. It's a
book about trusting your instincts and "thinking without thinking," and in one chapter, Gladwell discusses Dr. John Gottman,
a famous researcher from Seattle who Gladwell says can pre-
dict with 93.6 percent accuracy whether or not a couple will get
divorced simply by witnessing an interaction between them.

We paused the audiobook. We both wanted to take in that concept, the idea that a couple's success or failure in marriage could be predicted. We wondered what Dr. Gottman would say about us, about our friends. It was awful to imagine that some of them might be destined for divorce, and that even Tony and I could potentially split up at some point. We held hands, reaffirmed our love for each other, and then continued to listen. From that moment on, we've taken our treatment of each other much more seriously.

What's remarkable is that Dr. Gottman, in his now famous "Love Lab," isn't just making a guess about couples' futures. He and his team have been studying couples for decades, and they've figured out the key factors that help couples stay married as well as those factors that can lead to divorce. He calls the divorce factors "the Four Horsemen of the Apocalypse." They are contempt, criticism, defensiveness, and stonewalling. There is a lot to learn about each of them, but the thing that prompted Tony and me to immediately change our behavior was what Gottman said about a seemingly harmless bit of body language: the eye roll.

Rolling my eyes is a move I learned in elementary school and mastered in high school. It communicated perfectly without a single word that I thought my mom had no idea what she was talking about and I had no intention of listening. Now, I learned, it could potentially communicate the very same thing to my husband—and maybe even start us on a path toward divorce. Body language is a powerful communicator, and it is precisely a roll of the eyes that Dr. Gottman is trained to notice and categorize as an indication of the presence of contempt.

Contempt has a subtle way of entering a relationship. It's often when couples are conflict-avoidant or passive-aggressive or both that contemptuous feelings begin to take root. When a person who is feeling slighted decides, maybe as a defense mechanism, to bury that feeling rather than bring it into the open, they begin down this path of division. Contempt is a sentiment of superiority. When you start to look down on your partner and believe yourself to be better than they are, it's easy to think subtle, disrespectful thoughts about them: *He's stupid, lazy, and incompetent*, or *She's the worst!* These messages are then expressed in direct or subtle actions like ignoring, dismissing, and eye rolling. Contempt is the opposite of respect. Respect says, "I appreciate you," while contempt says, "I'm better than you."

What we need to do is recognize that feeling of contempt as a little seed that gets planted in our minds. We can choose to nurture that seed by rolling our eyes and being passive-aggressive, or we can dig it up by choosing to find ways to appreciate and respect our partners instead. All the little ways we communicate with each other matter. They build up into patterns and set the tone for how we treat each other overall. You may think rolling your eyes is just a mindless reaction and wonder how you can even help it when your spouse says something ridiculous. But if you knew—and now you do—that a seemingly no-big-deal eye roll was actually indicative of a deeper disrespect for your spouse, could you stop yourself from doing it? The truth is that you do have control over your behaviors, even the little ones.

Because contempt can be so subtle, it's easy to get away with allowing these feelings to fester. But when we ask God to search our hearts and show us the evil in them, we can quickly see where we're feeling bitter and contemptuous toward each other. If you notice how often you're tempted to roll your eyes, you may also begin to notice how often you're using other types of body language to communicate any disrespect and unkindness that may be lurking beneath the surface. Noticing your error, then taking responsibility, and finally choosing to replace those feelings with respect and appreciation could make a drastic difference in your interactions.

For Discussion:

1   Take a few minutes apart to write down three things you appreciate about each other. Come back together and take turns sharing.

2   What do you think it is about contempt that makes it so detrimental to marriages?

3   Conflict-avoidant and passive-aggressive couples are at a greater risk for experiencing contempt in their marriage. How do you think entering into conflict honestly can help prevent contempt from taking over?

4   Pray. Thank God that he searches our hearts and shows us what is hiding underneath the surface. Ask him to show you where you need to dig up bitterness and contempt to make way for respect and appreciation for each other.

A Fruitful Garden

*The Holy Spirit produces a different kind of
fruit: unconditional love, joy, peace, patience,
kindheartedness, goodness, faithfulness,
gentleness, and self-control.*
—Galatians 5:22–23

Sometimes I forget how spoiled we are. I walk through the produce section of my grocery store and get so picky about the fruits
and vegetables I'm willing to spend money on—no bruises on
the apples, no flimsy broccoli, no scraped-up zucchini. I want the
best, so I fill my basket with the prettiest fruits and vegetables,
put it all on a conveyor belt, swipe my debit card, and come home
full of pride over my selections. I don't give much thought to how
this food was grown or shipped or even how long it's been in the
store separated from its original source. If I were responsible for
growing my own fruits and vegetables to feed my family, I think
we might have a serious vitamin deficiency. I'd have to do a whole
lot of research—what grows in our northwestern climate, what
the soil should be like, when to plant what—and then at some
point, I'd have to actually plant something, and nurture it, and

wait until my fruits and vegetables were ripe enough to eat. When I think about all that, I become really grateful for grocery stores.

In life, we often want to partake of the good fruit without putting in any of the labor. We want to pick and choose what we'd like in our life—a fantastic partner, a happy home, a great job—seal the deal, and live happily ever after. But life is much more like a garden than a grocery store. Our marriages require us to engage in the work before we ever see good fruit.

I love that the Bible describes the characteristics God would refine in us as "fruit." The first several times I read Galatians 5, I focused on the characteristics themselves: love, joy, peace, patience, kindheartedness, goodness, faithfulness, gentleness, and self-control. I thought, *Yes! I need more of that in my life.* It turns out, the fruit itself is not the point—it's the work that goes into making it. I can't just grab the fruits I want like I would in the produce department. This fruit is not a product to consume; it's evidence. It's the proof that the Holy Spirit is already at work in our lives. It doesn't simply appear.

Ordinary fruit like apples and oranges begin as a seed and are nurtured and cultivated in the right environment. The young tree is usually guided by a stake in the ground that holds it upright, teaching it the direction it should go. As it matures, the tree is pruned, its dead branches removed so that they don't zap nutrients away from the growing fruit. And when the fruit begins to form, it is inspected, tenderly nurtured, and allowed to grow until it's perfectly ripe.

In the same way, if we want the characteristics mentioned in Galatians to be evidenced in our life and marriage, we must cultivate them. Great marriages may appear effortless on the outside, but each couple knows the work that goes into the fantastic relationship they have. It's a wonderful cycle: We work hard for things and then we see the beautiful results of our efforts, which makes us more willing to continue the work, which makes us appreciate the results of our work even more. The work always comes first.

It can be tempting to sit back and relax after your wedding day. Let life come to you, indulge in any natural selfishness, and don't worry about behaviors like blaming, avoiding, and defensiveness. But the result of those actions will be a mediocre marriage—or worse, one you dread. If, however, you want a marriage full of the fruit of the Holy Spirit, you'll have to step into the dirt and get to work. When you find you lack some of the characteristics you're aiming for, ask yourself, "Have I let God prune this area of my life? Have I allowed the Holy Spirit to nurture the seeds that were once planted? Is there a friend or mentor I can trust to be like a stake in the ground leading and guiding me in the way I should grow?" If this all sounds like more work than you're willing to do, then, like the gardener who gives up and allows weeds to overtake the garden, you may never enjoy the beauty that could grow in your own marriage.

For Discussion:

1   Read Matthew 13:1–23. Jesus is preaching a parable using seeds as an illustration. How do you think his story and its explanation connect with the verses in Galatians 5 about the fruits of the Spirit?

2   As you've done the work of coming together to read these
    devotionals and spending time in conversation and prayer,
    have you noticed any good fruit coming out of your lives?
    What rewards have you seen from your work?

3   With regard to the fruits of the Spirit discussed in
    Galatians (unconditional love, joy, peace, patience, kind-
    heartedness, goodness, faithfulness, gentleness, and
    self-control), which trait(s) do you think the Holy Spirit is
    working on cultivating more of in your life? What does that
    look like?

4   Pray. Thank God for being a good and faithful gardener,
    planting seeds of holiness in our lives and bringing about
    good fruit. Pray that you would see opportunities to be
    pruned, to cut away the characteristics that produce bad
    fruit in your lives, and to be gracious to each other through
    this hard and important work.

Impossible Decisions

> *Whoever pulls away from others to focus solely on his own desires disregards any sense of sound judgment. A fool never delights in true knowledge but only wants to express what's on his mind.*
> *—Proverbs 18:1-2*

While wonderful and magical, parenthood also brings a level of tension to my life that my pre-parent self could not imagine. Our first baby brought joy. Our second brought delight and companionship for the first. Our third brought wonder—and the need for a larger vehicle. Suddenly, we were asking ourselves the same question many modern American families have asked themselves: Shall we, or shall we not, succumb to the minivan?

Tony said, "We shall not!"

I said, "We shall!"

We were at an impasse for months. When it comes to these big decisions, it feels like whoever is holding the "no" or "not yet" card has the power. This can make the person holding the "yes" or "let's do this" card feel disregarded and overlooked.

Those feelings alone can make coming to an agreement even more difficult than the actual issue. These are *not* "don't fight over the butter" issues. They are deeply rooted heart issues, and they need to be unearthed and paid attention to, not ignored and dismissed.

When we're at odds over something big, the division seeps into other areas of our lives. But what if it's not about my way versus your way? What if there's a better way? Each of us assumes that our ideas are the best ideas. Since this is true, getting through an impasse requires at least one person to try to see the issue from the other person's perspective.

So, finally, instead of approaching Tony and saying, "We need to talk," which can instantly put him on edge, I took a slightly different approach: I asked if I could listen to him. Beginning with the desire to listen to my husband sets my own heart on a course of trying to understand him. I said, "Tony, I'd like a chance to listen to you. It seems like you really don't want a minivan, and I'd like to hear your ideas and understand more about it."

Driving to yet another dealership just two weeks before our third baby arrived, I looked over at my husband and remembered, *I love him. I know he's reasonable and wants nothing more than to take care of his family. I can trust that whatever we do, we will do it as a team.* I didn't know that day we'd be going home in a new car we both loved *that wasn't a minivan*, but I trusted him. I trusted us.

I always want my husband to know he is valued and heard. We are partners, even when we disagree, and I don't want to be his adversary. Also, when I engage in listening to him and taking in his perspective, he's more inclined to want to listen to my opinions, too. Depending on the topic, we may not come to complete agreement in one conversation (or ever). But I'm also learning that complete agreement isn't necessarily the goal. With that in mind, here are four tips for facing impossible decisions:

Four Ways to Face Impossible Decisions

1   **Set a time to listen.** Setting a time to listen shows genuine respect for the other person, giving them full freedom to think their own thoughts and have their own opinions. To listen well is to express understanding, affirming that their ideas make sense. It takes away the adversarial atmosphere in resolving conflicts and creates an atmosphere of friendship.

2   **Decide where you can be flexible.** Again, because you each believe your perspectives to be valid, decide what areas of the big decision you can be flexible with. Maybe it's the timing—do you need to agree right now? Maybe you can be flexible in some other area. Be open to that.

3   **Work toward understanding.** Sometimes these decisions are so heavy that the solution is not going to come from just one conversation. Instead of making the decision your primary focus, make understanding and honoring each other your goal. If the decision feels pressing, set a time to come together and make a final choice after you both have had some time to think about the other's perspective. Don't be like the fool in Proverbs who only wants to express what's on his mind.

4   **Show gratitude.** Whatever decision you come to, or if you don't come to one at all, it's vital that both of you feel heard and acknowledged. Thank your spouse for entering into this tough situation with you, for pushing through the tension, and for showing love and respect by acknowledging your differences in opinion.

When making your own impossible decisions, remember to give your spouse the benefit of the doubt, listen to where they're coming from, and practice being flexible.

For Discussion:

1   Think about the toughest decision you've made together. Do you both agree on which decision it was? Talk about what comes to mind about the decision.

2   If you could change anything about the way you handled that tough decision, what would it be?

3   Which of the four ways to face impossible decisions seems most important to you? Why?

4   Pray. Thank God that he promises to give us wisdom when we humble ourselves and ask for it. If you're facing a tough decision now, pray for his leading and guidance, as well as unity between the two of you. If you aren't facing a tough decision currently, thank him for the peace you enjoy and ask him to prepare your hearts to listen to one another when those tough decisions come.

Week 44

Let's Date!

> *But above all these [things], put on love!*
> *Love is the perfect tie to bind these together.*
> —Colossians 3:14

When Tony and I first started seeing each other, most of our dates were over breakfast. Sitting with a cup of coffee, waiting for warm hash browns and eggs Benedict in the light of day, seemed like a good way to actually get to know each other. We were definitely falling in love, high on limerence (the psychological term for those powerful feelings of infatuation we experience when a relationship is new), and often those breakfast dates would lead to a long walk through the city, then a deli-style picnic lunch, and on into the afternoon. We couldn't get enough of each other.

It's limerence that makes people crave each other obsessively, longing for reciprocation, hardly able to think of anything else. It's a state of mind, and, as most discover, it's temporary. You can think of limerence like love goggles through which you see your intended as darn near perfect and your relationship as pure magic. When limerence fades, which it always does, we begin to see each other more honestly and the real work of living and loving begins.

In the beginning of our relationship, Tony and I didn't need anyone to remind us how important it was to go on dates. Because of that limerence state of mind, being alone together was the only thing we wanted to do. Our bond was being formed. But once we were married, we preferred sleeping in to getting up early to go to breakfast. We ate breakfast in our pajamas on the couch, bingeing on HGTV. The limerence was fading. That's not a bad thing. In many ways, it's a good thing; we were beginning to experience each other as we really were, finding new ways to grow and connect. But after the birth of our first baby, we started to realize the value in setting aside time for each other by going on dates.

Your marriage can certainly survive without regular date nights, but who wants to merely survive? If we want to thrive, we must find ways to regularly connect. A date is really just a vehicle for reconnecting. For Tony and me, that might look like setting out a board game and some good snacks after the kids have gone to bed, leaving our phones in the other room. If Tony's in a busy freelance season, we might meet in the kitchen late at night to make second dinner, a meal just for two, the way we did when we were married but didn't yet have kids. We move around each other, grabbing ingredients and talking and laughing and catching up without our darling interrupters grabbing our calves the way they do during our usual dinnertime hustle. Sometimes reconnecting does look like leaving the house together on a real actual date. When we do, there are a few things we try to remember to make the most of our time together.

Making the Most of Your Date

1   **Schedule it.** Nothing delights me more than seeing the
    words "Date Night" on our calendar. I know it means Tony
    has secured a babysitter and wants to spend time with me.
    Looking forward to something is part of the fun of a date. If
    you don't plan it and schedule it, going on a date is a lot less
    likely to happen.

2   **Make connecting the goal.** Most of us are so attached to
    our devices during the day that it takes real discipline to
    put our phones away when we're out. When you make
    connecting the goal, you remind yourselves that the texts
    and notifications can wait. You're sitting across from the
    most important person in your life, and they deserve your
    full attention.

3   **Make time to dream.** If we're not purposeful, we can spend
    the entire evening discussing logistics, bills, and school
    schedules. But there's much more to us than our daily roles
    and responsibilities. Practice listening and engaging over
    each other's hopes and dreams. Ask each other questions
    like: What are you hoping for lately? What have you been
    craving, culinarily or otherwise? If we could take a week-
    end away, where would you want to go?

I often hear couples lament, wishing their marriage could be
like it was in the early days of dating. What they fail to see is that
when limerence fades, it makes way for a new and deeper kind of
love. Over time, as our souls commingle toward unity, we develop
a love based on mutuality and kindness, a love based on the
faithful acts of building a life together. Though infatuation and

obsession fade, curiosity and connection don't have to. Our souls within us are infinite, so there are an infinite number of ways to explore each other and continue to grow. Dating won't bring back those new-relationship feelings. But whether you go out or stay in, you have to be purposeful about the time you spend together. When we're in a routine for too long, we stop paying close attention to each other. If soul-bonding connections are going to be made, they aren't going to be made in the humdrum of the daily autopilot. We need opportunities to see each other and to be seen for who we really are.

For Discussion:

1   What does dating each other look like now, compared to the early days of your relationship?

2   Besides dating, what are some other ways the two of you regularly connect with each other?

3   The Bible calls us toward unity and away from divisiveness. When would you say you feel the most united with each other?

4   Pray. Thank God that his Spirit is one of unity. Pray that he would continue to bring unity and connection in your marriage, and that anything that would cause division or disconnection would be uprooted. Pray that, as you look for ways to have those soul-bonding connections, he would be there in the midst of you.

Poured Out

> *Though He was in the form of God,*
> *He chose not to cling to equality with God;*
> *But He poured Himself out to fill a vessel brand new;*
> *a servant in form and a man indeed.*
> *—Philippians 2:6–7*

One night, I stopped by a friend's house to drop off a book for her to borrow. She invited me in for a glass of wine, and we started to catch up. At the time, we had a lot in common. We'd both been married about the same amount of time, both had little girls about the same age, and both worked full time. It was past her daughter's bedtime; her husband was watching the news in another room. She asked what my husband was up to, and I shared that he had probably just given Claire a bath and was putting her to bed.

Then the conversation turned. She clenched her teeth and said, "I swear, other than bath time, I do everything around here! It's like he thinks these things just happen by themselves. I mean,

I work, and so do you, and so do our husbands. But still, I'm stuck doing most of the chores. I'm sick of it!"

"Whoa," I said. "Have you talked to your husband about it?"

"No, he never wants to talk. He comes home and turns the TV on immediately. A few weeks ago, I stopped doing his laundry. I don't even know if he's noticed. He can just take care of it himself. I'm about to stop washing his dishes, too, except I don't want the kitchen to be a mess when people come over."

At that point, I wasn't sure what to say. She was clearly hurt and mad, but she wasn't asking for my input. Honestly, it's one of those conversations that haunts me. I wish I'd been brave enough to share with her how important it is to at least try talking to your spouse when you're upset. I wish I'd told her how destructive it is to be passive-aggressive, to simply stop doing things you used to do without having any kind of discussion about it. But I could tell, even then, that the chores weren't the real problem.

Married people often fight about chores, but I think what we really struggle with is fairness, equality, and appreciation. Yes, we should be looking for ways to even out the load of unpaid work. We should practice asking each other humbly for what we need and being honest when we are feeling overwhelmed. Because we are all equal in the sight of God, we should be working together as battle buddies and co-warriors. But if we make total equality the goal, we're going to feel bitterness and resentment rise up when seasons change and one spouse needs to put in more time at work than the other, or when one spouse gets sick and can't do as much around the house.

Look at Philippians 2:6–7 again. Jesus "chose not to cling to equality with God" but rather "poured himself out" as "a servant."

If anyone could ever claim "That's not fair!" it was Jesus Christ. And he did express how overwhelmed he was to God the Father, when he prayed in the Garden of Gethsemane, "Father, if You are willing, take this cup away from me" (Luke 22:42). He carried the weight of all our sin on his shoulders, even though he himself was sinless. So, I thank God that he was more concerned about his relationship with us, his adopted sons and daughters, than about what was fair.

While there will always be unpaid work and shared responsibilities to take care of, we don't need to let these be what divides us in our marriage. Look for ways to serve one another, ask for help when you need it, and remember that, in the end, you're on the same team.

For Discussion:

1   Each of you take a piece of paper and spend a few minutes writing out a list of all the things you handle most of the time around the house. Then, with a same-team mind-set, show each other your lists.

2   Were you surprised by the list your partner wrote? Take a deep breath and begin talking about how you can be more of a team when it comes to the unpaid work in your life. Are there areas you'd like help with?

3   Most of us want to live in a world that is fair, but we don't often complain when the scales tip in our favor. Instead of making complete fairness the goal, how can you begin to think about the division of responsibilities in your home?

4   Pray. Thank God that he demonstrated his love through sacrifice, and that Jesus did not claim what was fair but rather laid down his life for each one of us. Pray that you would be reminded of his sacrifice as you do the work to become battle buddies and co-warriors and ultimately make sacrifices for one another.

Generous Love

> *Share what you have with the saints, so they lack*
> *nothing; take every opportunity to open your life*
> *and home to others.*
> —*Romans 12:13*

There's something about sharing food with my children that I simply cannot refuse. I just can't bring myself to look at their sweet faces and say, "No, you may not eat my apple slices. They are for me, not you." Tony often steps in to say, "Let Mommy eat her own dinner," because he knows I won't refuse them my food. I can't. It makes me smile to watch their tiny hands reaching over, the way they bashfully look into my eyes and humbly ask, even though they're pretty sure I'm going to say yes. I share with them happily, because my girls mean more to me than my last bite of food. I can't imagine withholding something of so little value to me from people whose value to me is immeasurable.

Tony and I wrote our own wedding vows, and in them we each promised, "I will not withhold any good thing from you." It was an expression of generosity. A promise to share any goodness we receive for ourselves with each other. Just like with my kids at dinner, if Tony wants something from me, my hands are open to him. Whatever goodness I possess I will not hoard for myself. Like we tell our kids, "We share because everything is a gift." The Bible says, "Every good gift bestowed, every perfect gift received comes to us from above, courtesy of the Father of lights" (James 1:17). We truly believe everything we have is a gift. Even the things we've earned and worked hard for, we earned by work that was entrusted to us, through gifts and talents we're responsible for nurturing and developing. If everything is a gift, who are we to withhold things from one another?

Generosity is a cornerstone of our faith. But generosity is not just about sharing physical resources. To be generous in a marriage is to give each other the benefit of the doubt, to be quick to forgive, to do your spouse a favor without mentioning what a hassle it was for you. Generosity does not expect reciprocity. Generosity doesn't keep score. Generosity expands our hearts. Some think they can't afford to be generous with money or anything else because they see these things as static and finite: *If I give to you, I won't have enough for me.* But when you know your source is infinite, it's easy to give and give some more. When we give, we inadvertently receive traces of grace in our hearts, footprints that generosity leaves behind. We think better of people when we give to them. We think better of our situations when we see that we have something to share with others. It's the act of giving that increases our gratitude and helps us see the expansiveness of life.

When you're generous in your marriage, you send a message to your partner that says, "You are valuable to me. You are more important than anything else I would hold onto." Marriage is the process of letting go of yourself, letting go of your ego. Marriage is about giving all of yourself to someone else, withholding no good thing from one another. Tony and I have found the most happiness when we're giving to each other, our family, and our marriage, instead of trying to see what we can get out of it. When I find myself frustrated that I'm not getting what I want, it serves as a great reminder to look for what I've put into our marriage lately. Have I sacrificed? Have I done something out of the ordinary just for my husband? Have I been kind and thoughtful? Have I been encouraging? There is always more that I can give, and in the giving, love grows.

For Discussion:

1 I like to share food. Tony doesn't. Sometimes I generously allow him to eat his own meal; sometimes he generously shares his meal with me. How do the two of you handle sharing?

2 When have you been on the receiving end of someone else's generosity? How did that make you feel?

3 In what areas of your life and marriage could you be more generous?

4 Pray. Thank God for his generosity, for the gifts he's blessed you with. Pray that he would expand your trust in him and, in so doing, expand your ability to be generous to each other and to those around you.

Week 47

The Hard Times That Remain

> *Do not forget to rejoice, for hope is always just around the corner. Hold up through the hard times that are coming, and devote yourselves to prayer.*
> —Romans 12:12

In our first year of marriage, Tony and I argued about the wet towels he left on the bed and why I never put my dirty clothes in the hamper. (What if I can get one more wear out of those jeans before I do laundry?) Little things. That's what that first year is about: discovery. Your expectations and dreams are confronted with reality, and those things never line up completely. We didn't know then that some of the things we argued and disagreed about, some of the things that hurt, would become the things that we still can't come to terms with 10 years into our marriage.

Some problems in your marriage just aren't going to be solved. These are perpetual problems, and every couple has them. You fight about them, but nothing seems to change. You plead your case, you listen to your spouse's, you may even reach some kind of agreement or compromise, but then, before too long, you're arguing about it all over again.

Tony and I spent our eighth anniversary date at a tapas bar discussing our perpetual problem. I won't go into too much detail about the disagreement itself, because I don't think this detail is necessary for you to understand the concept of navigating perpetual problems in your own marriage, and because we're still working through it and we believe it's important to protect the vulnerable parts of our relationship. What I will tell you is that the drive to dinner was awkward. The night before, we'd had a fight about our perpetual problem. I don't know what Tony was thinking at this point, but I can tell you I was wondering if we were just going to try to move on or if we were going to talk about it again. Sometimes it's hard to know if bringing up the same issue over and over can really do anybody any good.

Before long, tiny beef skewers and drinks were set in front of us, and when our eyes met across the table it was clear that we weren't going to ignore something that felt so important. We didn't fight, but we did rehash the previous night's fight and tried our best to listen to each other's perspective. I cried, he held my hand and told me he loved me. We still had no real resolution, and we decided we wouldn't reach one without some serious help.

That night, we made our first appointment with a marriage counselor. Weeks later, on the drive home from that first appointment, we digested together how things had gone. "I don't know," Tony said to me. "I guess I thought there would be more to it than just sitting and talking. Isn't there something else she can do? I've heard of this light therapy, or, like, hypnosis. I'm just not sure that sitting and talking is going to be all that helpful."

I laughed a little at his assessment. He wasn't sure sitting and talking would be all that helpful? I pointed out that he'd shared two significant thoughts with the therapist that I'd never heard him say before. What he said gave me insight into our struggle and helped me understand him a little more. Our perpetual problem hadn't been solved, but we were able to see each other from an angle we hadn't previously thought to look from.

It may be difficult to believe, but people in happy and healthy marriages experience ongoing disagreements and still find ways to love and honor each other. One key is to discover if your problem is solvable or if you've reached what some psychologists refer to as "gridlock." You know you're gridlocked if you've done your best to speak to each other, to listen well, and to be kind and respectful about the issue, but you still find that the issue remains. This is where Tony and I have been.

We would love to find a solution for our perpetual problem, but we both acknowledge that we may never do so. We're on a journey with the help of our therapist and marriage mentors toward better understanding. Little by little, the tension and pressure we were feeling before has been released. It no longer seems like a hazy fog over our marriage that we hope will just go away. Because we're actively pursuing each other through counseling and conversation, the haze dissipates, communication becomes clearer, and our love for each other grows.

We have a good marriage, but that doesn't mean it's not hard sometimes. And when our marriage is hard, that doesn't mean it's not still good. Some of the issues in your marriage are here to stay. The trick is not always to solve your perpetual problems, but to learn how to live with them, to honor and respect each other, and to grow in understanding and connection.

For Discussion:

1   It can take time, sometimes years, to discover your own perpetual problems. Can you name yours?

2   Read Romans 12:9–13 together. How do you think the attitudes and characteristics discussed in these verses could help you navigate perpetual problems?

3   Have you considered marriage counseling before? What benefits might come from having a third-party perspective?

4   Pray. Thank God that, no matter how many times we falter and fail, he does not throw in the towel on his relationship with us. Pray for clarity and wisdom so that you may have a better understanding of one another. Ask God to reveal to you any next steps you may need to take in addressing perpetual problems as a team. Thank him for the gift of a partner to wrestle through tough situations with, and for the hope he has placed in your hearts.

Direct Your Passions

> *Timothy, run away from youthful desires. Instead,*
> *direct your passion to chasing after righteousness,*
> *faithfulness, love, and peace, along with those who*
> *call upon the Lord with pure hearts.*
> *—2 Timothy 2:22*

I often think back to what first drew me to my husband. I mean,
he's very good looking, but I know a lot of good-looking people.
What really caught my eye was watching him play guitar with
his band on stage. I couldn't have articulated it then, but it was
more than just a groupie crush. I loved that he was creative and
willing to share his music in public. I loved that he was confident
and comfortable on stage, that he knew how to have fun with
his friends. That was 15 years ago, but all of that is still true of
him today.

Sometimes, without even realizing it, people lose themselves
once they get married. We let go of our hobbies and interests. We
don't make time to pursue the things that once made us come

alive. In an attempt to build a life with another person, we let go of the things we loved as individuals. Then we find ourselves frustrated with the pace of our lives, overwhelmed by our responsibilities. We feel stuck. That frustration seeps into all of our interactions, and usually it's our partners who get the brunt of it. We start looking at them and thinking, *I'm not happy. My partner is not making me happy.*

The truth is, your partner was never meant to make you happy. Your marriage is not meant to be the sole source of your joy and contentment. Marriage is a long, lovely conversation—a journey to discover and be discovered. As we grow and change, it's vital that we continue to pursue the things we once loved and make new discoveries along the way. Otherwise, we put unnecessary pressure on our marriage to fulfill us in ways it was never meant to.

Not only do we need to keep looking for ways to engage our individual interests, but we also need to create an atmosphere where our beloveds feel the same freedom and encouragement to pursue the things that excite them. Marriage works best when both partners bring their full selves into the relationship, and we can't do that if we've stopped exploring the things that engage our passions and interests. Sometimes we need to let go of the things we once loved, simply because our priorities change when we get married. But you can maintain your hobbies and have a healthy marriage if you can keep these few things in mind:

Three Ways to Keep Your Hobbies *and* Your Marriage

1 **Courtesy.** Exploring your individual interests without courtesy for your family will definitely bring tension. I love spending time with my friends, but if I plan a weekend away with them without first checking in with my husband, that's not going to work. I need to be courteous about the needs of my family when making my own plans.

2 **Transparency.** This is about honesty. If Tony knows he's going to play video games for 45 minutes but tells me he's only going to take 15 minutes because I'm more likely to give the green light to that, that's dishonest. Whenever you know you'll be taking a significant amount of time away from your family, you should be truthful and realistic about it. Expectation without clear communication leads to conflict, so it's best to be clear and honest.

3 **Priorities.** Whatever your hobbies and interests are, they should not take priority over your marriage and family. It would not have been appropriate for me to take a week away at a writing retreat a few weeks after giving birth, leaving my husband alone to take care of the kids. It would not be okay with me if Tony committed to a band that played shows four nights a week. Our first priority is always each other, and no other hobby or interest should push our marriage into second place.

About a month before Tony proposed to me, he gave notice to the band he'd played with for seven years. He was pursuing

God and pursuing me, and he believed that the amount of time he spent with the band wasn't helping him move forward in the areas of his life he valued most. I was stunned. I really loved watching him play and loved the guys he played with. But, as Paul exhorted Timothy, sometimes we have to let go of the things we loved in our youth in order to move on to a better and more fruitful life.

Thankfully, Tony has found new ways to write and play music, and to enjoy his life. If we want to avoid unnecessary resentment, we must be able to explore our individual interests. We just have to make sure those interests don't bump our partners out of their rightful place as our most important human relationship.

For Discussion:

1   Before you were married, what were the things you were interested in? Did you stop pursuing those things or have you continued?

2   If you had the time and money, what new interest would you pursue?

3   Are there ways you can adjust your life so that each of you can spend time on your individual interests?

4   Pray. Thank God for leading and guiding your life. Ask him to reveal to you the passions he's put in your heart that he wants you to pursue, together or individually. Ask him for the grace to allow each other to be invigorated by pursuing passions so that you can bring your full selves into your marriage.

Week 49

The Wise Counsel of Friends

> *The heart is delighted by the fragrance of oil and*
> *sweet perfumes, and in just the same way, the soul*
> *is sweetened by the wise counsel of a friend.*
> —*Proverbs 27:9*

After Tony and I made our vows to one another on our wedding day, our pastor asked us to face our friends and family. Then he asked them, "Will all of you witnessing these promises do all you can support Tony and Michelle in their marriage?" They responded, "We will."

Friendship and community are a vital part of marriage that many people overlook. We must make time for friendships. Your partner was never meant to fulfill all of your relational needs. You need community. We all do. We were created as relational, communal beings. Our triune God gives us a glimpse at the vital importance of community as he exists in the three-person Trinity: Father, Son, and Holy Spirit, all together, all at once, all the time. When we isolate ourselves from healthy community and look only to our marriage for comfort, wisdom, and joy, we miss out on the great gifts of friendship.

Standing beside me on our wedding day were two of my dearest friends, Katy and Natalie. They committed, along with the rest of our wedding guests, to support Tony and me, and to this day they've taken their vows to us quite seriously. Natalie was standing right next to Tony, praying over me and supporting us both, during the birth of our first child. When we came home from the hospital the next day, Katy was waiting for us, having just flown from Washington to Wisconsin to make us meals, wash our dishes, and do our laundry for our first 10 days as parents. I cannot imagine having to endure the stress and confusion of the beginning days of parenthood without our faithful friends cheering us on in the most tangible ways.

Our friends have seen us through some crazy life transitions, hired us to work when times were tight, made us meals when we've been sick, participated in our shenanigans, and provided invaluable wisdom and even more invaluable babysitting hours. When there's friction between Tony and me, it's our friends who point us back to each other and help us regain the perspective that we really do have a good marriage. Science backs this up; one study by researcher Rose McDermott found that "attending to the health of one's friends' marriages may serve to support and enhance the durability of one's own relationship."

Not all friendships are equally beneficial to your marriage. If your friends are toxic—inconsiderate, insulting, self-centered, breaking the law, disregarding their own marriages, constantly bringing you down—then you've got some evaluating to do. Everyone has bad days and bad moments. I've said hurtful things and stuck my foot in my mouth on more than one occasion. But I'm not talking about off-handed remarks and innocent mistakes here. I'm talking about consistently toxic character. It's important for you and for your marriage that you do your best to maintain a healthy distance from toxic friendships. If any of your friendships make your spouse uncomfortable, it's certainly worth considering their feelings about that friendship. Assuming your marriage isn't abusive, healthy friendships will always point you back toward your marriage; they won't try to pull you apart.

Quality friendships, just like marriage, require us to invest in them. If you want to have quality friendships, you need to be a quality friend. Being a better friend to those you admire and respect, investing your time and generosity in sincere, kind people, will help you attract healthy friendships. Be the kind of friend you hope to have. Practice being interested in those around you. Practice being a better listener. It's easy to get in a routine with our spouses and forget to make time for friendships, but we must make room in our lives for these important relationships.

Tony knows my tendency is to be a homebody, so he encourages me to go out with my girlfriends and to invest time in these relationships and put myself in the position to receive love and encouragement from them. (Another of McDermott's findings was that "social isolation" from friendship networks didn't help prevent divorce.) Tony and I know that giving each other the space to be loving and supportive friends to others always benefits our marriage. Making sure you've built and kept a close community of people is one of the best things you can do to ensure your marriage lasts.

For Discussion:

1. Do you know who your partner's three closest friends are? Share with each other the qualities that make those friendships so valuable.

2. Read: John 15:9–17. Do you believe you have a friendship with Jesus? Talk with each other about what these verses mean to each of you.

3. Sharing a meal is a wonderful way to engage with your friends. Make plans together to invite others to your home to eat a meal together. (Ordering pizza is perfectly acceptable. The point is to make space to connect.)

4. Pray. Thank God that he is the best example of a friend, laying down his life for us. Thank him for the community and friendships you have, and ask him to show you how you can empower each other to be better and more present friends to those in your life.

Support One Another

> *So support one another. Keep building each other up as you have been doing.*
> *—1 Thessalonians 5:11*

Marriage is more than divvying up chores and sidestepping conflict. One of the blessings of marriage is that you have someone in your corner encouraging you to pursue your dreams—and you also get to be that person for someone else. There are times we get so bogged down by the dailies that we forget to dream at all. But having hope and imagining what your future will be like together creates a stronger bond between you, so it's important not to let your dreams fall out of sight.

It's not easy to get through life with a dream in your heart, with all the doubt and discouragement the rest of the world will throw your way. Once we have our dreams in sight, we need our partner, our best friend, to believe in us. There are many ways we can offer support. Before we can fuel each other on toward our dreams, it's important to identify what different types of supportive behavior really look like and which situations they're most helpful in.

The Four Types of Supportive Behavior

1 **Emotional support.** Emotional support is all about empathy. It might take the form of offering physical comfort, listening well, or holding your partner's hand. If you've ever had a draining day or experienced disappointment as you pursue your goals, knowing that your spouse is there to support you emotionally can carry you through. We all have times when this is the best and maybe the only kind of support we need.

2 **Esteem support.** Esteem support boosts your partner's confidence. Verbally giving your partner specific encouragement shows them that you're paying attention. This is the one I need most often. When my husband tells me he admires me and believes in me, I feel immensely supported. His confidence in me gives me confidence in myself and makes me feel closer to him.

3 **Informational support.** Informational support is a way to offer and utilize each other's unique perspectives. It usually involves giving advice, offering your expertise, and gathering information to help your partner. Since Tony and I are good at different things, this comes up nearly every day. I'll often tell him about an idea and ask him if he can help me execute it. He's a brilliant designer and is always

happy to either show me how to create the thing I have in mind or take care of it for me. To my delight, he seeks support from me in this way also. He'll ask me to proofread or offer insight on an e-mail to a client because he trusts the way I interact with people, especially in writing. Sharing insights is a wonderful way to support each other.

4 **Tangible support.** Tangible support might be the most practical. We all feel supported when we know our partners will take on extra responsibilities to free us up to tackle something important to us. It happens around here when Tony offers to clean up the kitchen after dinner so I can jump into the office to take care of some things that are on my mind. I can return the favor when I push him out of the house with his laptop for the evening while I stay home with our girls. This kind of teamwork mentality is essential.

When you're in a rut, it's easy to let the days pass without purpose. But we're called to be purposeful with our lives, to be awake to the opportunities and pursue what God has given us to do, and to develop the gifts and talents we've been given. If we really want to live life to the fullest, it is essential that we know how to dream and then share our dreams with our partners.

Whatever our dreams may be, all of us need to be supported. Tony is usually quick with the tangible support, and I need to remember to ask for esteem support when all I want is encouragement. He always gets it when I finally use words to say what I'm thinking. His support is so valuable to me that I never want to overlook it. I also want to keep being supportive of him in the ways he needs. One of the great glories of married life is the opportunity to support one another and build your dreams together. Work together to build the adventurous life you both want, and you'll build a life of fulfillment.

For Discussion:

1   Ask your partner, "What have you been daydreaming about lately?"

2   Read 1 Thessalonians 5. In it, Paul talks a lot about those who are "asleep" and those who are "awake." What do you think the differences are? Would you say you're living awake to your life's purpose, or have you been sleeping?

3   Of the four supportive behaviors, which would you say you need most right now? How might that change your day-to-day interactions?

4   Pray. Thank God for the gifts and talents he's blessed you with. Ask the Holy Spirit to guide you toward the dreams in your heart. Pray that you would see how to help each other realize what God has given each of you and how your dreams fit together for his purposes.

The Inner Struggle

> *Any place where you find jealousy and selfish*
> *ambition, you will discover chaos and evil thriving*
> *under its rule. Heavenly wisdom centers on purity,*
> *peace, gentleness, deference, mercy, and other*
> *good fruits untainted by hypocrisy.*
> —James 3:16–17

My daughters have a complicated relationship with each other. Most of the time, they're sweet to the point that they start giggling and hugging each other in public. The three of them, Claire, Nora, and Alice, all with their big eyes and curly hair, give off this delightful *Little Women* vibe that draws people in. They, of course, love the oohs and aaahs from strangers, so the sweetness becomes a self-fulfilling cycle. They do something sweet, a stranger notices and compliments them, and they love the compliments, so they do more sweet things.

At home, however, no strangers are around to compliment them on their every twirl and smile, so they tend to get a little less sweet. The giggling and hugging turns into snatching and screaming. They yell and push and fight and, as their mom, it's my job to step in and referee. Breaking up a fight between people with less than six years of life experience is a ridiculous task. Facts are irrelevant. It's all blaming, screaming, and stomping. Somehow I'm responsible for bringing peace to this war zone. It's complicated.

The thing is, this is the kind of behavior we expect from children. But, as adults, when our own tempers flare, we revert right back to our preschooler selves, doing things like blaming, screaming, and stomping. We develop our routines of conflict, and if we don't examine them—examine the *way* we fight and not just what we're fighting about—we can get stuck in a divisive cycle of chaos. We're complicated beings. Our natural selfishness makes it difficult to be in a growing and thriving relationship with anyone else, especially if we haven't first discovered and dealt with our own motives.

Anger, for instance, is a secondary emotion. Anger is a cover for deeper and stronger emotions like fear and pain. We react by losing our temper, but if we can pause and take a deep breath in the midst of our anger, the anger itself can become a clue. After learning this, I noticed that I often get angry when I'm trying to load the kids into the car. I can never figure out why they move so slowly. And the buckles! Why are there so many buckles, and why are the straps always tangled? The longer it takes us to leave the house, the angrier I feel. So I paused one day as I felt the anger rising and asked myself, *Is there something that hurts? Is there something I'm afraid of?* When I really thought about where that anger was coming from, I realized I was afraid of being late, afraid that getting my daughter to school late would reflect poorly on me as her mother. I was afraid of being judged.

Now, it took more time and reflection for me to figure that out than it took for me to write those words. Most of us don't give ourselves or each other the time to think and reflect. When we're angry, it's easier to point fingers and criticize each other than to look inward and take responsibility for our own behavior. But if we want peace and unity in our marriages, we have to resist the temptation to treat our partners like enemies.

Relationships are complicated and full of struggle. But if we're willing to struggle with each other instead of against each other, conflict can be productive and even healing. Struggling together means you're both willing to grow, and growth doesn't happen without some resistance and pain. Just as our muscles grow through resistance, our love for each other grows through struggle and pain. Getting to the other side of hardship, we look back and we see that we are not broken, but stronger together.

Relationships are complicated because we often have more feelings than we have words to describe them to someone else. Even when we do have words, our vocabulary is limited to our awareness. That is to say, as much as we can, we should endeavor to increase our awareness of ourselves, find out what it is that truly drives and motivates us, and then learn to describe those things to the person we want to be in a relationship with. We must be able to tell our own story and identify our own triggers if we have any hope of ever being understood by anyone else.

This is why counseling and therapy are so useful. In what other context will you have a witness while you verbally process all that you discover? In what other setting can you be safely guided away from the lies you've always believed about yourself? But submitting yourself to counseling, to receiving insight from a third party, requires both maturity and vulnerability, and many times we'd prefer to take the easy route and keep blaming each other instead of finding a better way.

Relationships are complicated, but when we can look both inward at ourselves and outward at the way we impact others, we can get better at living with and loving those around us.

For Discussion:

1   Most adults find that, even if they've truly grown and matured in many areas of their lives, they revert back to old patterns when they spend time with their siblings and parents. Have you found this to be true in your lives? What does that look like?

2   Have you ever taken a personality test, for work or otherwise? What did that test teach you about yourself? How has that influenced your behavior and relationships?

3   Have you learned anything about yourself since you got married? How did you make that discovery?

4   Pray. Thank God for being willing to wrestle with us and carry us through our struggles. Pray that, as you create a safety net in your marriage, you would have the grace to allow each other time to pause and reflect on what's going on beneath the surface when you fight. Pray that your conflicts would lead to understanding and peace instead of division.

Walt and Nancy

> *Ultimately it does not matter whether we are here or*
> *gone; our purpose stays fixed, and that is to please Him.*
> *—2 Corinthians 5:9*

It was the text I dreaded: "We are moving him to hospice today."

Our dear friend Walt had been battling lung cancer for a long time. When I received his daughter's text, we knew we needed to prepare to say goodbye.

I responded, "We would like to come visit. Would that be okay?"

Walt's daughter Lynn met us in the hallway at the hospice house and instantly burst into tears. Walt had exhaled for the last time about 30 minutes before we arrived. Tony and I wrapped our arms around her and stood there weeping together. We made our way into the room where he lay, still and pale. Sitting nearby was Nancy, his wife of 38 years. We hugged and caught each other's tears on our shoulders. She thanked us for being there and said, "Sometimes things aren't fair. It's a fact of life, but it is such a hard fact."

Walt's body was there, but it was clear to all of us that he was not. His kindness, his generosity, and his humble smile were not lying in that bed. Nancy and I sat together holding hands. "I don't want to go home," she said. "I don't want to be there without him. I've never been without him in 38 years."

There's a trend to modernize traditional wedding vows to make them more realistic. Some have opted for "as long as our love shall last" in lieu of "until death do us part." But Tony and I look at couples like Walt and Nancy, and we see that it's commitment, not emotion, that keeps a couple together. It is a desire to serve one another, to choose the well-being of the person beside you before your own, that keeps a marriage strong.

Walt and Nancy would always rather be together than apart. And here we were, witnessing the culmination of their vows, in which they promised to be together until death separated them. Yet, even with her husband's passing, Nancy is not separated from Walt. Their faith, they always told us, was the centrifugal force binding them together.

In 2 Corinthians 5:6–9, Paul and Timothy write:

> *In light of this, we live with a daring passion and know that our time spent in this body is also time we are not present with the Lord. The path we walk is charted by faith, not by what we see with our eyes. There is no doubt that we live with a daring passion, but in the end we prefer to be gone from this body so that we can be at home with the Lord. Ultimately it does not matter whether we are here or gone; our purpose stays fixed, and that is to please Him.*

This is how Walt and Nancy taught us to live: passionately, purposefully, and looking for ways to please God. Nancy's adoration of her husband, her commitment to their life together, will not fade. They committed their lives to one another, not once and for all, but every single day.

We interviewed them a few years ago, and Walt shared this advice with us: "Don't miss an opportunity to be with your wife! Staying married is not all there is. At our age, we know couples who have been married 30 years or more, but they really aren't together. They live in separate bedrooms, some in separate houses, vacation separately, and don't have any shared interests. Nancy and I spend a lot of time together, even doing things the other might not love so much. You know, shopping is not on my list of favorite activities, but I go with her so I can be near her. We take drives together just to talk."

This is it. I want for myself and for you a marriage that transcends time and mortality. A lifetime of love and arguments and obstacles overcome. I want a legacy that causes a younger couple to ask, "What was their secret? How did they do it?" and I want the answer to simply be "With love and kindness, patience and understanding, commitment and forgiveness, they were able to stay married."

For Discussion:

1   Have you experienced the death of someone close to you? What was that like for you?

2   Walt shared that he went shopping just to be near Nancy. What are some of the things you do, not because you

love them but because you want to be near your partner?

3   What are characteristics of your marriage others might find admirable?

4   Pray. Thank God that, through the sacrifice of his own son Jesus, death is not the end of our story. Ask the Holy Spirit to help you live your life together with passion and purpose, and for your union to be a light inspiring those around you. Thank God for the gift he has given you in each other.

Resources

Marriage is a long, lovely conversation in which we get to learn and grow for the rest of our lives. The following are resources to help with the journey.

Books

Bell, Rob, and Kristen Bell. *The Zimzum of Love: A New Way of Understanding Marriage*. San Francisco, CA: HarperOne, 2014.

Brown, Brené. *Daring Greatly: How the Courage to Be Vulnerable Transforms the Way We Live, Love, Parent, and Lead*. New York: Gotham, 2012.

Chapman, Gary D. *The Five Love Languages: How to Express Heartfelt Commitment to Your Mate*. Chicago. IL: Northfield Pub., 1995.

Cloud, Henry, and John Sims Townsend. *Boundaries in Marriage*. Grand Rapids, MI: Zondervan Publishing House, 1999.

Gottman, John Mordechai, and Nan Silver. *The Seven Principles for Making Marriage Work*. 2nd ed. New York: Crown, 2015.

Johnson, Susan M. *Hold Me Tight: Seven Conversations for a Lifetime of Love*. New York: Little, Brown, 2008.

Parrott, Les, and Leslie L. Parrott. *The Good Fight: How Conflict Can Bring You Closer*. Brentwood, TN: Worthy, 2013.

Websites

#staymarried: Hope, stories, and resources for couples who want to stay married—staymarriedblog.com

The Gottman Institute: Research-based approach to strengthening relationships—www.gottman.com

Marriage 365: Helping Couples Connect—marriage365.org

Prepare Enrich: The leading relationship inventory and skill-building program—www.prepare-enrich.com

Dr. Tina Schermer Sellers: Rediscovering Intimacy—tinaschermersellers.com

References

Augsburger, David. *Caring Enough to Hear and Be Heard.*
Ventura, CA: Regal Books, 1982. Accessed via Google Books
January 17, 2017.

Brittle, Zach. "K Is for Kissing." The Gottman Relationship Blog.
May 28, 2014. www.gottman.com/blog/k-is-for-kissing/.

Cashmore, Judith, and Rita Shackel. "The Long-Term Effects of
Childhood Sexual Abuse." CFCA Paper, No. 11. The Australian
Institute of Family Studies. January 2013. aifs.gov.au/cfca
/publications/long-term-effects-child-sexual-abuse/export.

Chillot, Rick. "The Power of Touch." *Psychology Today.*
March 11, 2013. www.psychologytoday.com/articles/201303
/the-power-touch.

Clark University. "New Clark Poll: 18- to 29-Year-Olds Are
Traditional about Roles in Sex, Marriage, and Raising
Children." Accessed January 1, 2017. www.clarku.edu/article
/new-clark-poll-18-29-year-olds-are-traditional-about-roles
-sex-marriage-and-raising-children.

Covey, Stephen M. R. *The Speed of Trust: The One Thing That Changes Everything*. New York: Free Press, 2006.

Dennison, Renée Peltz. "Are Children of Divorce Doomed to Fail?" *Psychology Today*. August 2, 2014. www.psychologytoday.com /blog/heart-the-matter/201408/are-children-divorce-doomed-fail.

Eldredge, John, and Stasi Eldredge. *Captivating: Unveiling the Mysteries of a Woman's Soul*. Nashville, TN: Thomas Nelson, Inc., 2005.

Fottrell, Quentin. "Americans Take Half of Their Paid Vacation, but Chinese Take Less." *MarketWatch*. September 11, 2015. www.marketwatch.com/story/americans-only-take-half-of-their -paid-vacation-2014-04-03.

Gottman, John. *The Seven Principles for Making Marriage Work*. 2nd ed. New York: Harmony Books, 2015.

Ledbetter, Sheri. "Chapman University Researcher Leads Team to Examine What Keeps Passion Alive in Long-term Relationships." *Chapman University Press Room*. February 9, 2016. blogs.chapman.edu/press-room/2016/02/09/chapman-university -researcher-leads-team-to-examine-what-keeps-passion -alive-in-long-term-relationships/.

McDermott, Rose, James Fowler, and Nicholas Christakis. "Breaking Up Is Hard to Do, Unless Everyone Else Is Doing It Too: Social Network Effects on Divorce in a Longitudinal Sample." *Social Forces: A Scientific Medium of Social Study and Interpretation* 92, no. 2 (2013): 491–519. www.ncbi.nlm.nih.gov/pmc/articles /PMC3990282/.

The Holy Bible. English Standard Version. BibleGateway.com. https://www.biblegateway.com/versions/English-Standard -Version-ESV-Bible/#copy.

————. The Living Bible. BibleGateway.com. https://www.bible gateway.com/versions/The-Living-Bible-TLB/#copy.

————. The Voice. Nashville, TN: Thomas Nelson, Inc. 2012.

"This Holiday in Dance." The Ellen DeGeneres Show. NBC, Burbank, CA. Television Broadcast. December 16, 2016. www.ellentv.com/episodes/jim-parsons-cass-mccombs-sabre -norris/.

Twain, Mark. Mark Twain to Gertrude Natkin. 1906. In *New York Public Library Digital Collections*. digitalcollections.nypl.org/items /53b4cf90-7739-0132-f12c-58d385a7b928.

VanderWeele, Tyler J. "Religious Service Attendance, Marriage, and Health." *Family Studies.* November 29, 2016. family-studies.org /religious-service-attendance-marriage-and-health/.

Whisman, Mark A., Lisa A. Uebelacker, and Lauren M. Weinstock. "Psychopathology and Marital Satisfaction: The Importance of Evaluating Both Partners." *Journal of Consulting and Clinical Psychology* 72, no. 5 (2004): 830–838. doi:10.1037/0022-006X.72.5.830.

Wolpert, Stuart. "Here Is What Real Commitment to Your Marriage Means." UCLA Newsroom. February 1, 2012. Accessed January 4, 2017. newsroom.ucla.edu/releases/here-is-what-real -commitment-to-228064.

Index

Acknowledgments

I'd always imagined writing a book alone in a cabin with an ocean view. In reality, this book was written in the midst of my everyday life as a wife raising three daughters. It absolutely would not have been possible without my tribe: people who have come alongside me to teach me, encourage me, edit my work, care for my kids, remind me to eat, and bring me wine.

To Katie Saesan, thank you for sharing your love of language with me. Your talent as an editor has been an incredible blessing. Thank you, Jonah and Skip, for sharing dear Katie with me; she is such a treasure.

To Rich and Barbara Butler, thank you for investing in us at the beginning of our marriage and for cheering us on ever since. Tony and I are still aiming to be just like you when we grow up.

To Ryan and Michelle Meeks of Eastlake Church, David and Rindy Nelson of Great Lakes Church, and Jesse and Marisa Butterworth of Rain City Church. Thank you for risking everything to launch these incredible communities of hope and authenticity that have nurtured and challenged me over the years. They have also been the birthplaces of my dearest friendships.

To Katy Davies, Natalie Winnett, Sarah Nienaber, Emily Higginson, Karen Jussel, Kristen Engen, and Heidi Denham, thank you for standing with me on my wedding day and all the days before and after. You are the most incredible wives to your husbands, mothers to your children, and sisters to me.

To our Supper Clubs and Growth Groups in the Midwest and the Pacific Northwest and to my Anam Caras, thank you for teaching me about the power of community and the blessing of allowing myself to be fully known.

To Drs. John and Julie Gottman, Michael Fulwiler, and the team at The Gottman Institute, thank you for your decades of research and for encouraging me to keep writing and sharing.

To Nana K. Twumasi and the team at Callisto Media, thank you for believing in me and working tirelessly to take this book from a dream to a reality.

To the #staymarried community, this book is yours! Thank you for reading, listening, and sharing with others. Your faith in me and commitment to grow in your own relationships were the inspiration for this book in the first place.

To Tony, Claire, Nora, and Alice, thank you for filling my home with music and laughter and for pushing me to write this book. I love you.

About the Author

MICHELLE PETERSON loves love! Growing up with a single mother, she didn't know if she'd recognize long-lasting love for herself or if she'd ever find it. Once she got married, she realized that love was not something to find, but something to cultivate, nurture, and grow. After witnessing far too many of her dear friends experience the devastating pain of divorce, she set out to understand as much as she could about what it takes to make a marriage last and then to share that knowledge with everyone she knew.

Michelle began as the author of dozens of tweets ending with the hashtag: #staymarried. Those tweets evolved into what is now *The #staymarried Blog* and *The #staymarried Podcast* on which she works together with her husband to serve hundreds of thousands of couples around the world with her approachable encouragements and research-based tools.

Michelle lives with her husband, Tony, and their three daughters: Claire, Nora, and Alice. You can find more of her writing and speaking at *staymarriedblog.com*.

CPSIA information can be obtained
at www.ICGtesting.com
Printed in the USA
LVHW051603050221
678367LV00002B/2

9 781939 754097